English Study Guides
with Answer Key

H O L T
Economics

HOLT, RINEHART AND WINSTON

A Harcourt Education Company

Austin • Orlando • Chicago • New York • Toronto • London • San Diego

Printed in the United States of America

ISBN 0-03-067518-9

4 5 6 7 023 09 08 07 06

Contents

HOLT ECONOMICS ENGLISH STUDY GUIDES WITH ANSWER KEY

This study guide provides brief summaries of each of the textbook's sections. A series of questions are provided at the end of each summary.

CHAPTER 1

WHAT IS ECONOMICS?

STUDY GUIDE 1.1

SUMMARY

Economics is the study of the choices that people make to satisfy their needs and wants. A need is anything that is necessary for survival, such as food, clothing, and shelter. Wants are goods and services that people consume beyond what is necessary for survival. Goods are physical objects that can be purchased, and services are actions or activities performed for a fee. People who supply goods and services are called producers, and people who purchase goods and services are called consumers.

Economic decisions involve resources. A resource is anything that can be used to satisfy a consumer's want or need. Resources that can be used to produce goods and services are known as factors of production. Economists generally recognize four categories of resources: natural resources, human resources, capital resources, and entrepreneurship.

REVIEW QUESTIONS

1. Define the following terms: economics, microeconomics, macroeconomics, factors of production, natural resources, human resources, capital resources, entrepreneurship.

2. Why is learning about economics an important part of making responsible choices?

3. What factors do economists consider to be economic resources?

4. What is the relationship between consumers and producers?

5. **Thinking and Writing Critically**
   If you were an entrepreneur, what business or product would you create, and what would be some of the risks involved in creating it?

6. **Applying** Economic Resources
   Explain how technology is used to improve the creation of goods and services. Provide an example, stating what product is being made and how technology is used in making it.

CHAPTER 1

WHAT IS ECONOMICS?

STUDY GUIDE 1.2

SUMMARY

Scarcity is the basic fact of economic life. Human needs and wants are always greater than the resources available to satisfy them. Therefore, choices must be made concerning how to best use the limited resources available. To make these choices, an economic system or society must answer the three basic economic questions: what to produce, how to produce, and for whom to produce.

Once an economic system has answered the questions of what, how, and for whom to produce, production must be carried out as effectively as possible. To reach the highest possible levels of productivity, producers may rely on division of labor and specialization.

REVIEW QUESTIONS

1. Define the following terms: scarcity, allocate, productivity, efficiency, division of labor, specialization.

2. Why is scarcity an economic problem?

3. What decisions about production must be made to allocate resources effectively?

4. What two factors can increase productivity?

5. **Thinking and Writing Critically**
   Consider a limited resource, such as money, and describe how having a limited amount of that resource has affected a decision.

6. **Applying Productivity**
   How does the division of labor and specialization influence productivity in your household or classes? How could you improve efficiency to increase productivity?

CHAPTER 1

WHAT IS ECONOMICS?

STUDY GUIDE 1.3

SUMMARY

Scarcity requires choice. Economists call the sacrifice of one choice for another a trade-off. They call the next-best choice an opportunity cost. The production possibilities curve can be used to analyze the trade-offs and opportunity costs involved in producing specific combinations of goods and services. A production possibilities curve assumes that the amount of available resources and the state of technology will not change during the period being studied and that resources are used as efficiently as possible. Changes in resources or technology result in a shift of the entire production possibilities curve either to the right or to the left.

REVIEW QUESTIONS

1. Define the following terms: trade-off, opportunity cost, production possibilities curve.

2. How do economic resources determine production possibilities?

3. What does the production possibilities curve indicate?

4. Why is the production possibilities curve a helpful tool in making production decisions?

5. **Thinking and Writing Critically**
   What trade-offs have you made recently? What were the opportunity costs? What influenced your decision?

6. **Applying Production Possibilities**
   A computer company must decide whether to make more desktop computers or laptops. How might the company determine what it should focus on building? What must the company assume will not change during the period being studied? Give an example of one production possibility.

CHAPTER 1

WHAT IS ECONOMICS?

STUDY GUIDE 1.4

SUMMARY

Producers and consumers distribute goods and services through a system of exchange. Forms of exchange include barter and purchasing goods and services with money or credit.

In an exchange, goods and services are assigned a value, or a worth that can be expressed in terms of money. This price is determined by the product's scarcity and utility.

Exchange reduces self-sufficiency and encourages interdependence, linking different regions and economic actors. Interdependence, in turn, encourages specialization, as individuals, industries, and regions concentrate on producing specific goods and services to meet particular needs and wants.

REVIEW QUESTIONS

1. Define the following terms: exchange, barter, money, credit, value, utility, self-sufficiency, interdependence.

2. What can producers learn from the exchange process?

3. What is the basis for determining value, and why is it important?

4. What effect does exchange have on self-sufficiency and interdependence?

5. **Thinking and Writing Critically**
   People in the U.S. exchange products by bartering, using money, or paying with credit. Which form of exchange do you think is the most efficient? Consider the advantages and disadvantages of using each type of exchange. Explain your answer.

6. **Applying** Exchange, Money, & Interdependence
   Do you think that the Internet has made exchange easier or more difficult? Support your answer.

CHAPTER 2 — ECONOMIC SYSTEMS

SUMMARY

Nations—as well as individuals—respond to scarcity and answer the three basic economic questions of what to produce, how to produce, and for whom to produce. A nation's answers to these questions are determined by its economic system. An economic system is the way that a nation or society is organized to produce and distribute goods and services. Economists have identified four types of economic systems: traditional, command, market, and mixed. In the modern world, all economies are mixed.

Traditional economies depend on long-established patterns of behavior and belief. Command economies rely on government decision making and control of resources. Market economies allow individuals to control and allocate resources. Market economies also rely on self-interest and incentives.

Mixed economies have elements of traditional, command, and market models. Because mixed economies vary in their characteristics, economists classify them by the degree to which government controls the economy. Nations whose economies are closest to the pure command model are said to practice authoritarian socialism, or communism. Nations whose economies are closest to the pure market model are said to practice capitalism. Nations whose systems fall somewhere in between are said to practice democratic socialism.

REVIEW QUESTIONS

1. Define the following terms: traditional economy, command economy, market economy, market, self-interest, incentive, mixed economy, authoritarian socialism, communism, capitalism, democratic socialism.

2. What is the purpose of an economic system?

3. How is an economic system classified, and which system describes all economies?

4. How does self-interest benefit a market economy?

5. **Thinking and Writing Critically**
   Why do you think all economies in the modern world are mixed? Consider the different types of economic systems and how they operate. Explain your answer.

6. **Applying** Economic Systems
   Describe a time when incentives affected your work. Did they have a positive or negative effect? How?

CHAPTER 2

ECONOMIC SYSTEMS

STUDY GUIDE 2.2

SUMMARY

The economic system of the United States leans toward the market model. The fact that there is some government involvement and regulation, however, means that the U.S. economy is not a pure market model. Because the economic system of the United States is based on the freedom to make choices, it is often referred to as a free-enterprise system.

In the United States, individuals have the right to own private property and enter into contracts, make individual choices, engage in competition, and make decisions based on self-interest. Only a limited amount of government regulation and intervention exists in the U.S. economy.

Economists use the circular-flow model to show how resources, products, and payments are exchanged in the U.S. free-enterprise system. The product market represents all of the exchanges of goods and services in the economy. The resource market represents the exchange of natural, human, and capital resources in the economy.

REVIEW QUESTIONS

1. Define the following terms: free enterprise, private property, contracts, competition, voluntary exchange, product market, resource market, income.

2. What makes the U.S. a free-enterprise economic system?

3. What roles do producers, consumers, and the government play in the U.S. economy?

4. What does the circular-flow model indicate to economists?

5. **Thinking and Writing Critically**
   What are the elements of a free-enterprise economy? Find examples of each based on your own experience.

6. **Applying** Economic Systems
   In your own words, explain how the Internet can be considered a product and promoter of a free-enterprise economy. Find examples using the Internet.

CHAPTER 2   ## ECONOMIC SYSTEMS

SUMMARY

The above features of the free-enterprise system assist the economy in reaching its six main goals. These goals are economic freedom, efficiency, equity, security, stability, and growth. Economic systems must assign priorities to these goals by determining where to use scarce resources. Changes in circumstances can cause these goals to take different priorities at different times. Different groups within a nation also can disagree over how to achieve economic goals.

REVIEW QUESTIONS

1. Define the following terms: full employment, price stability, standard of living.

2. Why does a free-enterprise system have goals?

3. Define each of the six U.S. economic goals.

4. What can affect the prioritization of economic goals?

5. Thinking and Writing Critically
Think about your short- and long-term goals as they might relate to the economic objectives of the U.S. What goals are most important to you? How do you prioritize them? What types of situations have come up that have changed their level of importance?

6. Applying Economic Systems
Based on actual events, find examples of the six goals of the U.S. economy and discuss which goals are priorities now.

CHAPTER 3

DEMAND

STUDY GUIDE 3.1

SUMMARY

Demand is the quantity of a good or service that a consumer is willing and able to buy at various prices during a given time period. Price is one of the most important factors affecting demand. The law of demand states that an increase in price decreases the quantity demanded and that a decrease in price increases the quantity demanded, other things remaining the same.

The law of demand is explained by the income effect, the substitution effect, and diminishing marginal utility. The income effect appears when a change in price affects a person's purchasing ability. The substitution effect refers to the consumer's tendency to substitute a similar, lower-priced product for a more expensive one. Diminishing marginal utility reflects the decreasing satisfaction experienced as increasing amounts of a product are consumed.

Demand schedules and demand curves can chart how changes in price affect quantity demanded for a specific period of time. A demand curve slopes downward, reflecting the greater quantity that consumers will buy at lower prices. A change in price results in movement along the product's demand curve.

REVIEW QUESTIONS

1. Define the following terms: demand, quantity demand, law of demand, purchasing power, income effect, substitution effect, diminishing marginal utility, demand schedule, demand curve.

2. How does price affect demand?

3. What do income effect and substitution effect have in common?

4. How are demand schedules and demand curves related?

5. **Thinking and Writing Critically**
   Give an example of how your purchasing decisions have been influenced by price. What economic concept did you apply in making your choice?

6. **Applying Demand**
   Using the Internet or a newspaper, research the cost of computers from different sellers. What does the pricing tell you about the possible demand for the product?

CHAPTER 3

DEMAND

STUDY GUIDE 3.2

SUMMARY

Factors other than price can affect demand for a product over time, causing a shift in its demand curve. These shifts illustrate a change in demand at each and every price.

The determinants of demand are consumer tastes and preferences, market size, income, prices of related goods (substitute goods and complementary goods), and consumer expectations. Changes in market size can be caused by private business decisions such as new advertisements, government policy decisions, and new technology. Changes in any of the determinants of demand can produce an entirely new demand curve for a product.

REVIEW QUESTIONS

1. Define the following terms: determinants of demand, substitute goods, complementary goods.

2. What factors can shape market size?

3. How do changes in income contribute to shifts in demand?

4. Why do consumer expectations cause shifts in the demand curve?

5. **Thinking and Writing Critically**

   Describe a time when you have purchased substitute goods and complementary goods. What were they? What influenced your purchasing decisions in each case?

6. **Applying** Determinants of Demand

   Describe three ways that your personal economic decisions can affect the demand curve and how. What determinants of demand are your decisions based on?

CHAPTER 3 — DEMAND

SUMMARY

To determine whether a price change is in their best interest, business owners need to determine elasticity of demand. The demand for a product can be either elastic or inelastic. When a small change in a good's price causes a major change in the quantity demanded, demand is elastic. In contrast, inelastic demand occurs when a change in a good's price has little impact on the quantity demanded.

Goods that have elastic demand usually are not necessities, have readily available substitutes, and represent a large portion of consumers' income. The opposite is true for goods with inelastic demand. Elasticity of demand for a product can differ in specific and general markets.

The total-revenue test measures a product's elasticity of demand. A drop in total revenue following a price increase indicates elastic demand, while a rise in total revenue following a price increase indicates inelastic demand. Business owners try to find the price at which total revenue is maximized. This enables them to make pricing decisions that will earn the most revenue.

REVIEW QUESTIONS

1. Define the following terms: elasticity of demand, elastic demand, inelastic demand, total revenue.

2. How do business owners determine when a price change will benefit them?

3. What affects a product's elasticity?

4. What is the relationship between price and demand for products that have elastic demand?

5. **Thinking and Writing Critically**

   If you owned a business, why might you consider changing the price of the good or service you offered? Support your answer.

6. **Applying Supply**

   List two items with an elastic demand and two with an inelastic demand and offer reasons why the items fall in each category.

CHAPTER 4

SUPPLY

SUMMARY

Supply is the quantity of goods and services that producers offer at various possible prices during a given time period. Quantity supplied is the amount of a good or service that a producer is willing to offer at each particular price. The law of supply states that producers supply more goods and services when they can sell them at higher prices and fewer goods and services when they must sell them at lower prices.

Profit is the key motivation behind suppliers' behavior in providing goods to the marketplace. Supply schedules and supply curves are useful in charting the degree to which changes in prices affect quantities supplied.

The supply of goods can be either elastic or inelastic. When a small change in a product's price causes a major change in the quantity supplied, supply for the good is elastic. In contrast, inelastic supply occurs when a change in a product's price has little impact on the quantity supplied. A good usually has an elastic supply if it can be made quickly, inexpensively, and using a few, readily available resources. A good usually has inelastic supply if producing it requires a great deal of time, money, and resources that are not readily available.

REVIEW QUESTIONS

1. Define the following terms: supply, quantity supplied, law of supply, profit motive, profit, cost of production, supply schedule, supply curve, elasticity of supply.

2. What motivates producers to supply goods to sellers?

3. What two ways can suppliers determine product prices and the number of products to supply?

4. What is the difference between inelastic supply and elastic supply?

5. **Thinking and Writing Critically**
   Name an instance in which you offered a product or service. Why did you decide to offer it? What price did you charge, and how did you determine what to ask in exchange?

6. **Applying Supply**
   Give an example of an elastic supply and an inelastic supply. What qualities distinguish one from the other?

CHAPTER 4

SUPPLY

STUDY GUIDE 4.2

SUMMARY

Factors other than price can affect supply of a product over time, shifting the supply curve to the left or right. The determinants of supply are prices of resources, government tools, technology, competition, prices of related goods, and producer expectations.

Resources include raw materials and labor. A decrease in the price of resources causes an increase in supply. The opposite is true when an increase in the price of resources occurs. A tax hike causes a decrease in supply, while government subsidies increase supply. Loose government regulations tend to increase supply, while strict regulations tend to decrease supply. New technology and competition both usually increase supply. A change in the price of related goods can cause an increase or decrease in supply. Producer expectations also can cause an increase or decrease in supply.

REVIEW QUESTIONS

1. Define the following terms: determinants of supply, tax, subsidy, regulation.

2. What are the determinants of supply?

3. What happens when the price of a resource drops or rises?

4. In what ways do taxes, subsidies, and regulations cause the supply curve to shift?

5. **Thinking and Writing Critically**
   Look at the businesses in your community, perhaps in your local mall or shopping center. What businesses have high competition? What effect does competition have on supply and profits? What role does demand play in the success of the businesses?

6. **Applying** Production Technology & Supply
   Provide an example of how changes in technology affect new product supply. How do advances in technology lead to an increase in product offerings?

CHAPTER 4

SUPPLY

STUDY GUIDE 4.3

SUMMARY

Production decisions are affected by the need to maximize productivity and by the costs of production. When setting production levels, business owners must consider total product (all of the product a company makes in a given period of time), marginal product (the change in output generated by adding one more unit of input), and the law of diminishing returns (the fact that marginal and total product will decrease after a certain production level).

Making these production decisions also requires business owners to determine their fixed costs (production costs that do not change as the level of output changes), variable costs (costs that change as output changes), total costs (the sum of fixed and variable costs), and marginal costs (the costs of producing one more unit of output).

REVIEW QUESTIONS

1. Define the following terms: total product, marginal product, law of diminishing returns, fixed cost, depreciation, overhead, variable cost, total cost, marginal cost

2. What factors influence production decisions?

3. How do producers determine production levels?

4. What is meant by "input" and "output" in relation to the law of diminishing returns?

5. Thinking and Writing Critically

Explain how the law of diminishing returns applies to making beef stew. Describe, in economic terms, what happens if you double, triple, or quadruple the amount of one of the ingredients (input). Are the results the same when you quadruple the amount of beef as when you quadruple the amount of salt? What happens to the quality of the meal (output) in each instance?

6. Applying Production Decisions

Imagine that you own a sandwich-making business. What production decisions must you consider to make your business a success? Explain how each issue relates to your business.

PRICES

SUMMARY

In a free-enterprise market, prices are the main form of communication. They guide producers and consumers toward efficient compromises on production levels of goods and services.

The price system has several benefits. It provides producers and consumers with information about, as well as incentives to participate in, the marketplace. The price system also increases the number of choices available in markets and promotes the efficient use of resources. In addition, the price system is flexible enough to deal with sudden changes in supply and demand.

The price system does have limitations, however. It does not accurately assign the costs of externalities like pollution. Nor does it accurately distribute the costs and benefits of public goods like national defense. In addition, the system's occasional instability can make it difficult for producers and consumers to predict prices and plan for the future.

REVIEW QUESTIONS

1. Define the following terms: market failure, externality, public good.

2. Why are prices considered to be a type of language?

3. How do suppliers and consumers use the price system?

4. What is thought to be the price system's greatest asset, and what positive and negative effects does it have on the marketplace?

5. **Thinking and Writing Critically**
    How does the price system affect the way you make responsible purchasing decisions when you go shopping? What do you take into consideration when you shop for an item?

6. **Applying** Markets & Prices

    Suppose that floods damage crops in the Mississippi River valley. How does the price system respond to the damaged harvest? Does this response reflect a benefit or liability of the price system? Explain your answer.

CHAPTER 5 — PRICES

STUDY GUIDE 5.2

SUMMARY

The price system coordinates production decisions by steering producers and consumers toward market equilibrium. Market equilibrium occurs when the quantity of a product supplied and the quantity demanded are equal at the same price, meeting the needs of both producers and consumers.

To reach market equilibrium, producers must avoid surpluses and shortages. A surplus occurs when the quantity supplied is greater than the quantity demanded at a particular price. A shortage, on the other hand, occurs when the quantity demanded exceeds the quantity supplied at a given price.

A shift in either the demand or the supply curve can change a market's equilibrium point. These shifts may be the result of changes in consumer tastes and preferences, market size, income, prices of related goods, and consumer expectations. Changes in equilibrium may also stem from changes in government actions, technology, competition, producer expectations, and the prices of resources and related goods.

REVIEW QUESTIONS

1. Define the following terms: market equilibrium, surplus.

2. What helps drive market equilibrium?

3. What creates change in market equilibrium?

4. How can producers cope with surpluses and shortages, and how can they avoid them?

5. Thinking and Writing Critically

You are the manager of a book store. You must decide how many books to stock throughout the year. How do you determine how many books to stock and at what prices to sell them? Consider the problems of surplus and shortage that you might face throughout the year.

6. Applying Markets & Prices

What happens to the equilibrium point for pumpkins in September, October, and November? Draw graphs to help determine your answer and explain your results.

CHAPTER 5

PRICES

SUMMARY

The price system's limitations sometimes lead governments to intervene in the market. Governments may set prices by establishing price ceilings and price floors that are intended to protect producers and consumers from dramatic price swings. A price ceiling establishes a maximum price for a good or service, and a price floor establishes a minimum price.

Governments and other institutions also may ration goods that are in extremely short supply. Managing prices through price ceilings, price floors, and rationing interferes with the normal interaction between supply and demand, however, and can maintain or even worsen market imbalances. Additionally, many people feel that rationing is an unwise policy because it gives special treatment to some groups, is expensive, and encourages illegal sales through black markets.

REVIEW QUESTIONS

1. Define the following terms: price ceiling, price floor, minimum wage, rationing, black market.

2. What might government do to protect the market from becoming unstable?

3. How does government intervention in the market affect a free-enterprise system?

4. What is an example of a price ceiling and price floor as described in the section?

5. **Thinking and Writing Critically**

    Why do some people criticize rationing? What are their arguments? Do you agree or disagree and why? Consider the potential advantages and disadvantages of rationing.

6. **Applying** Markets & Prices

    Suppose that you have a part-time job and the government announces that the minimum wage will be eliminated. How might your income be affected by the removal of this price floor? How would you respond to changes in your income? Explain your answer.

CHAPTER 6 — MARKET STRUCTURES

STUDY GUIDE 6.1

SUMMARY

As a consumer, you tend to benefit most from highly competitive markets. These types of markets provide consumers with a range of products that are priced fairly and that reflect costs accurately. The forces of supply and demand promote competition by encouraging producers to supply consumers with a wide selection of goods and services.

Perfect competition is an ideal market structure in which buyers and sellers compete directly and fully under the laws of supply and demand. In general, perfect competition exists when four conditions are present: there are many buyers and sellers acting independently, sellers offer identical products, buyers are well informed about products, and sellers can enter or exit the market easily.

Monopolistic competition is much more common than perfect competition and differs from it in one important respect—sellers offer slightly different, rather than identical, products. In monopolistic competition, sellers exert some control over prices by differentiating their products through nonprice competition.

REVIEW QUESTIONS

1. Define the following terms: perfect competition, buyers, sellers, monopoly, monopolistic competition, differentiate, product differentiation, nonprice competition.

2. Why do highly competitive markets benefit consumers?

3. What is necessary for sellers to compete perfectly?

4. What characteristics do monopolistic competition and perfect competition share?

5. **Thinking and Writing Critically**
   Sellers try to differentiate their products in many ways. List three products you buy. How do manufacturers try to differentiate them? Is this market perfectly competitive? Explain.

6. **Applying** Competition & Market Structure
   Choose three products available for sale on the Internet. What type of competition exists for each one? Explain how each product fulfills the conditions necessary for either perfect or monopolistic competition.

CHAPTER 6   MARKET STRUCTURES

STUDY GUIDE 6.2

SUMMARY

In imperfectly competitive markets, fewer sellers offer fewer products and their prices are usually higher. The most common of these markets in the United States is the oligopoly. In oligopolies, a few large sellers control most of the production of a good or service through nonprice competition and interdependent pricing. In general, an oligopoly exists when three conditions are present: there are only a few large sellers, sellers offer identical or similar goods and services, and other sellers cannot enter the market easily. Sellers in an oligopolistic market have more control over prices than do sellers in a monopolistically competitive market.

In monopolies, a single seller controls the total production of a good or service. In general, a monopoly exists when three conditions are present: there is a single seller, no close substitute goods are available, and other sellers cannot enter the market easily. There are four main types of monopolies: natural, geographic, technological, and government. A single seller in a monopolistic market has a great deal of control over prices. However, this control over prices is limited somewhat by the forces of consumer demand, competition, and regulation.

REVIEW QUESTIONS

1. Define the following terms: oligopoly, interdependent pricing, price leadership, price war, collusion, cartel, natural monopolies, economies of scale, geographic monopolies, technological monopolies, patent, copyrights, government monopoly.

2. What are the effects of an imperfectly competitive structure?

3. How do oligopolies function?

4. In what ways can a seller create a monopoly over a market?

5. **Thinking and Writing Critically**
   Why might a group of sellers feel that a cartel would offer more opportunity for profits than would a monopoly?

6. **Applying Markets & Prices**
   Find an example of a seller that has a monopoly over a good or service. Why does it have a monopoly? Has it always been a monopoly? Explain your answer.

CHAPTER 6 **MARKET STRUCTURES**

STUDY GUIDE 6.3

SUMMARY

The United States in the late 1800s saw the era of big business, in which huge monopolies called trusts dominated the marketplace. At this time, the U.S. government had a laissez-faire policy toward business. However, in response to people's concerns about the amount of power these trusts had, the government passed several laws to protect consumers and ensure market competition. The Sherman Antitrust Act—later strengthened by the Clayton Antitrust Act—is the foundation of U.S. antitrust legislation. This act and subsequent legislation prohibit restraint of trade, the formation of monopolies, and unfair business practices such as price setting and price discrimination.

REVIEW QUESTIONS

1. Define the following terms: trusts, laissez-faire, antitrust legislation, price discrimination.

2. What motivated the U.S. government to interfere with "big business" in the 1880s?

3. What did the U.S. government do to end monopolies?

4. How does the government monitor unfair business practices?

5. Thinking and Writing Critically

What monopolies exist in your school? Consider how lunches, yearbooks, and other products are sold at your school.

6. Applying Competition & Market Structure

Identify three ways in which antitrust legislation might protect your family's economic interests.

CHAPTER 7 — BUSINESS ORGANIZATIONS

STUDY GUIDE 7.1

SUMMARY

The most common form of business organization is the sole proprietorship. A sole proprietorship relies on the work and organizational abilities of one person. Sole proprietorships are easy to start up, provide the single owner with full control of the business, and allow the owner to keep all the profits. There are several problems related to sole proprietorships. First, the proprietor has unlimited liability for business debt. Second, the proprietor is completely responsible for all aspects of the business. Third, sole proprietors often have difficulty raising capital. Fourth, a sole proprietorship lasts only as long as the proprietor is willing and able to maintain the business.

REVIEW QUESTIONS

1. Define the following terms: sole proprietorship, zoning law, liability, collateral, longevity.

2. Why would a business choose to be organized as a sole proprietorship?

3. What are some examples of occupations that are typically organized as sole proprietorships?

4. What risks do sole proprietorships face, and why are they risks?

5. **Thinking and Writing Critically**

   Imagine that you—as a student—are a sole proprietor who is paid in grades. Which advantages and disadvantages of sole proprietorships affect you and how?

6. **Applying** Economic Institutions & Incentives

   Imagine you are ready to open your own business. Would you choose to open a sole proprietorship? Explain your answer.

CHAPTER 7 — BUSINESS ORGANIZATIONS

STUDY GUIDE 7.2

SUMMARY

Partnerships spread the risk and workload of a company among partners. A partnership may be organized either as a general partnership or as a limited partnership.

Like sole proprietorships, partnerships are easy to set up. Unlike proprietorships, however, partnerships allow specialization and shared responsibility, shared decision-making, and shared business losses. Disadvantages for partnerships include unlimited liability, the potential for conflict, and a lack of longevity.

REVIEW QUESTIONS

1. Define the following terms: partnership, general partnership, limited partnership.

2. How do partnerships differ from sole proprietorships?

3. How are partnerships and sole proprietorships similar?

4. Why might some businesses choose to function as a general partnership and others choose a limited partnership?

5. **Thinking and Writing Critically**
   You are given the choice of working on a school project independently or with a group. Would you decide to act as a sole proprietor in working on the project or to enter a partnership with your schoolmates? Explain your answer, considering the benefits and risks associated with sole proprietorships and partnerships.

6. **Applying** Economic Institutions & Incentives
   If you were to start your own business, would you organize it as a general or limited partnership? Explain your answer.

CHAPTER 7 — BUSINESS ORGANIZATIONS

SUMMARY

A more complex type of business organization is the corporation. It is supervised by a board of directors. Legally, a corporation is treated as if it were an individual.

The corporation offers several advantages. First, stockholders and corporations have limited liability. Second, corporations permit the separation of ownership and management. Corporations also have relatively little trouble raising capital, and they offer longevity.

The disadvantages of corporations include expenses of establishing the business, strict government regulation, and a slow decision-making process. Additionally, shareholders are removed from daily company activities. Also, dividends are taxed twice—first as corporate profits and again as shareholder income.

REVIEW QUESTIONS

1. Define the following terms: corporations, articles of incorporation, corporate charter, board of directors, stock, shares, dividends, common stock, preferred stock, corporate bond, principal, interest.

2. What distinguishes corporations from sole proprietorships and partnerships?

3. What steps are involved in forming a corporation?

4. What about a corporation is appealing to investors?

5. **Thinking and Writing Critically**
   Consider the typical structure of a corporation. How might you consider your school to be a corporation? Who makes up the board of directors, the officers, and shareholders? What are the dividends?

6. **Applying** Economic Institutions & Incentives
   What types of decisions does a company's board of directors make? Using the Internet, search current news sources for an article illustrating a decision made by the board of directors of a corporation.

CHAPTER 7

BUSINESS ORGANIZATIONS

STUDY GUIDE 7.4

SUMMARY

Corporations are able to expand their operations by combining, or merging, with other firms. Horizontal combinations occur between companies that produce the same goods or services. Vertical combinations are mergers between companies involved in different phases of production of the same good or service. A conglomerate combination occurs between companies producing or marketing significantly different products.

Franchises, cooperatives, and nonprofit organizations are three additional types of business organization. In a franchise, one business agrees to let its name be used by another business—for a fee—to sell goods or services. A cooperative is a voluntary association of consumers or producers in some kind of business activity. Nonprofit organizations provide goods or services but do not seek profits for individual members.

REVIEW QUESTIONS

1. Define the following terms: merger, horizontal combination, vertical combination, conglomerate combination, subsidiaries, franchise, cooperatives, nonprofit organization.

2. In what ways can a corporation expand?

3. What are the advantages and disadvantages of corporate mergers?

4. What are characteristics of the different forms of cooperatives?

5. **Thinking and Writing Critically**
   Imagine you are the CEO of a corporation that makes personal computers, and you are considering buying another company. How do you determine whether a horizontal or vertical combination would benefit your company?

6. **Applying** Economic Institutions & Incentives
   Using the Internet, find an example of a subsidiary, franchise, cooperative, and nonprofit organization.

CHAPTER 8

LABOR AND UNIONS

STUDY GUIDE 8.1

SUMMARY

The U.S. labor force, which includes more than 130 million people, is made up of all people who are at least 16 years old and who are working or looking for work. These people are part of the civilian labor force.

Workers usually consider six main factors when they enter the labor force. These factors are wages, skill levels, working conditions, location, intrinsic rewards, and market trends.

The labor force has undergone numerous changes throughout the nation's history. Among these changes are a shift from a labor-intensive economy to a capital-intensive economy, increased numbers of women in the labor force, and higher levels of education among workers. Additionally, the government has passed a series of laws aimed at protecting workers from discrimination in hiring, promotion, and firing. These laws include the Equal Pay Act of 1963 and the Civil Rights Act of 1964. In addition, the 1938 Fair Labor Standards Act established the first minimum wage and protections for the rights of individual workers.

REVIEW QUESTIONS

1. Define the following terms: labor force, wage, intrinsic reward, derived demand, industrialization, capital-intensive, labor-intensive, affirmative action, quota.

2. Who makes up the civilian labor force?

3. How are wages subject to the laws of supply and demand?

4. What has the U.S. government done to protect workers?

5. **Thinking and Writing Critically**
   The face of the labor force has changed drastically since the early 1800s. For example, many women have entered the workplace. In what other ways has the labor force changed? Consider workers' skills, education, and job choices.

6. **Applying** Economic Institutions & Incentives
   Search the employment classifieds, using either the Internet or your local newspaper. What is the relationship between the education required for each job and the salary offered?

CHAPTER 8   **LABOR AND UNIONS**

STUDY GUIDE 8.2

SUMMARY

To secure their rights, many U.S. workers organized labor unions. These unions struggled for higher wages, improved working conditions, and job security for workers. Well-known unions have included the Knights of Labor, the American Federation of Labor, and the Congress of Industrial Organization. In 1955 the American Federation of Labor and the Congress of Industrial Organization merged to form the AFL–CIO. Today the AFL–CIO, with its more than 13 million members, is the largest and most powerful labor organization in the United States.

Labor union membership, however, has declined in recent years. This trend has resulted from several factors, including employer opposition, changes in employment patterns, and negative public opinion of unions. Unions have tried to face these challenges by cooperating more with employers and by addressing new issues of concern to workers.

The government's attitude toward unions has changed during the last century. In the late 1800s, the government regularly supported business owners. However, in the early 1900s—during times of social and political reform—activists were able to persuade the government to support unions by passing laws that protected the rights of workers. After 1940, the government again changed its position and passed new laws limiting the power of unions.

REVIEW QUESTIONS

1. Define the following terms: labor union, open shop, closed shop.

2. How did industrialization change the relationship between workers and employers, and what was the consequence?

3. What does AFL-CIO stand for and whom does it represent?

4. How has union membership changed in recent years and why?

5. Thinking and Writing Critically
The shift in employment trends has affected union participation. How have occupations changed? How have unions responded?

6. Applying Business Organizations & Labor Unions
Research a local union in your community. What is its membership size? What are its goals? Is it organized under another union? If so, which one? What type of workers does it represent? Document your findings.

CHAPTER 8

LABOR AND UNIONS

STUDY GUIDE 8.3

SUMMARY

Common labor contract issues between workers and management include wages and fringe benefits, working conditions and hours, job security, union security, and grievance procedures. Labor unions rely on collective bargaining, mediation, and arbitration to improve working conditions and wages for their members. If an agreement is not reached, unions resort to such tactics as strikes, picketing, boycotts, and coordinated campaigning. Management can counter these tactics by hiring replacement workers, introducing lockouts, and requesting injunctions.

REVIEW QUESTIONS

1. Define the following terms: fringe benefit, seniority, collective bargaining, mediation, arbitration, strike, primary boycott, secondary boycott, coordinated campaigning, lockout, injunction.

2. How do labor unions work to secure workers' rights?

3. What do a mediator and arbitrator have in common?

4. What can happen if contract negotiations between unions and management fail?

5. **Thinking and Writing Critically**
   Describe a dispute you have experienced with a friend or classmate. How did you try to resolve the argument? How did your methods resemble or differ from those used in union negotiations? What was the outcome?

6. **Applying** Business Organizations & Labor Unions
   Use current news sources to investigate strikes involving picketing, boycotts, and coordinated campaigning. Identify which businesses or industries are affected by the strikes. Of the three strike tactics, which, in your opinion, seems to be the most effective in initiating change? How does the effectiveness vary depending on the business or industry being targeted and the grievances being made? Support your answer.

SOURCES OF CAPITAL

SUMMARY

When people choose not to consume their disposable income, they are saving. In general, people save money for five major reasons: for major purchases, to pay large annual or semiannual bills, for unexpected expenses, for long-term expenses, and to amass wealth or leave an inheritance. By saving money, people gain financial security and interest, whether they rely on savings accounts or time deposits. Economists examine savings rates to determine the amount of money being saved throughout the economy.

REVIEW QUESTIONS

1. Define the following terms: disposable income, balance, liquidity, time deposits, maturity, savings rate.

2. Why is saving money important?

3. How does a regular savings account differ from a money market account?

4. What are the benefits of buying certificates of deposits and saving bonds?

5. **Thinking and Writing Critically**
   Explain how your personal savings rate is affected if you purchase a new stereo.

6. **Applying** Interest Rates
   Use current news sources to research how interest rates vary depending on whether banks are paying them or charging them. What did you find out?

CHAPTER 9   **SOURCES OF CAPITAL**   **STUDY GUIDE 9.2**

SUMMARY

Investing allows consumers to exchange their money for something of value, with the expectation of future profits. To meet their goals, investors develop financial plans that include spending and savings plans, investment plans, retirement plans, and estate plans. Investors who hope only that the value of their investments will grow with time are practicing financial investment, while investors who hope to increase their investment while creating new capital goods are practicing real investment. Real investment contributes to economic growth by creating new products and, indirectly, new jobs.

REVIEW QUESTIONS

1. Define the following terms: investment, budget, fixed expenses, flexible expenses, diversification, real investment, capital accumulation, infrastructure, venture capital.

2. What is a trade-off for investing?

3. Why is financial planning beneficial to making responsible financial decisions?

4. What type of investment stimulates economic growth and why?

5. **Thinking and Writing Critically**
   Estimate and list your fixed and flexible expenses and your monthly earnings, whether from a job or an allowance. How much money can you afford to save? What trade-offs can you make so you can increase the amount you save?

6. **Applying** Economic Institutions & Incentives
   What type of investment services are available over the Internet? What range of services is offered? Which services are free and which charge a fee? Conduct a search online for the word *investment* to help you find out. Outline your findings.

CHAPTER 9

SOURCES OF CAPITAL

STUDY GUIDE 9.3

SUMMARY

Investors buy stock to increase their profits, limit risk, and become owners of a corporation. Stocks are purchased from brokerage firms, which hold seats on stock markets such as the New York Stock Exchange (NYSE). Stocks not listed on stock exchanges can be purchased in the over-the-counter (OTC) market. Stock prices are determined by corporate finances, investor expectations, and external forces. Bonds offer lower returns than stocks, but because they are offered by federal, state, and local governments, they generally have less risk as well. Futures provide investors with the chance to collect future profits, although the high risks for businesses and investors discourage many people from participating. All of these securities are regulated by the federal government.

REVIEW QUESTIONS

1. Define the following terms: capital gain, capital loss, stock split, brokers, investment bank, bull market, bear market, yields, futures, prospectus.

2. In what ways can an investor profit from investing in stock?

3. What is a "blue chip" stock and why is it in high demand?

4. What form of investment offers the lowest risk and why?

5. Thinking and Writing Critically

Imagine you are researching how to invest in stock. You have the option to trade online or through a broker or an investment bank. Which do you choose and why?

6. Applying Economic Institutions & Incentives

Go online to the NYSE and NASDAQ Web sites, or review the stock prices listed in your local newspaper. From the information available, are we in a bull or bear market? How did you determine your answer?

SUMMARY

Borrowing and credit serve as other sources of financial capital. Borrowing enables people to enjoy their purchases now while paying for them later, spreading payments out over a period of months or years. Credit allows purchases to be made without an actual exchange of money. To develop a credit rating, a credit bureau evaluates a consumer's financial background on the basis of ability to pay, assets, and credit history. Consumers who abuse their credit may have difficulty paying debts and in some cases may be forced to declare bankruptcy.

There are economic benefits to credit as well. Credit can stimulate economic growth by enabling people to buy goods and services, thus promoting investment and job growth. Economic stability also can stem from credit, as supply rises to match increased demand. Increased supply requires producers to hire more workers, providing more people with incomes.

REVIEW QUESTIONS

1. Define the following terms: installment, credit rating, credit bureau, finance charge, annual percentage rate, usury, bankruptcy.

2. Why are the advantages and disadvantages of borrowing money? Using credit?

3. Why are credit ratings evaluated before individuals are approved for credit?

4. What effect can wisely used credit have on supply and demand?

5. **Thinking and Writing Critically**

   Why do you think people fall into credit debt? How can people overcome their debt and avoid future debt? Are any trade-offs involved in wise credit use? What are they?

6. **Applying** Economic Institutions & Incentives

   Investigate how finance charges vary on three different credit cards. Make a list to compare your findings. Be sure to name the bank offering the credit card, the type of credit card it is, and whether or not the finance charges are promotional.

CHAPTER 10 — ECONOMIC PERFORMANCE

SUMMARY

Macroeconomists use national income and product accounts (NIPAs) to measure the output and income of national economies. This process is known as national income accounting. The primary account used to measure a nation's output is gross domestic product (GDP), the total dollar value of all final goods and services produced within a given country's borders during one year. Other commonly used measures of a nation's economy are net domestic product, national income, personal income, and disposable personal income.

In computing GDP, economists use the output-expenditure model, which is the sum of a nation's personal consumption expenditures (C), gross private domestic investment (I), government purchases of goods and services (G), and net exports (X – M). Nominal GDP is GDP expressed in the current prices of the period being measured. Real GDP is GDP adjusted for the change in prices.

Because GDP is limited to market transactions and excludes nonmarket activities and the underground economy, it is only an approximate measure of a nation's total output. In addition, GDP does not differentiate between "good" and "bad" output and, as a result, is only an approximate measure of a nation's well-being.

REVIEW QUESTIONS

1. Define the following terms: national income accounting, gross domestic product, output-expenditure, personal consumption, gross investment, nominal GPD, real GPD, price index, underground economy, gross national product.

2. What three criteria must goods meet to be counted as part of GDP and why?

3. How is GDP adjusted for price increases?

4. Why did the U.S. replace gross national product GNP with GDP as a means for measuring economic production?

5. **Thinking and Writing Critically**
Provide an example of national, personal, and disposable personal income. Explain your answers.

6. **Applying** Gross Domestic Product
Identify one of the "goods" and "bads" overlooked by GDP. Why are they labeled "goods" and "bads"? What new measure of the economy do some economists suggest will account for these contributors?

CHAPTER 10

ECONOMIC PERFORMANCE

STUDY GUIDE 10.2

SUMMARY

Business cycles are fluctuations in economic activity that occur in a market system as measured by increases or decreases in real GDP. The business cycle is divided into four stages or phases: expansion, or recovery; peak; contraction, or recession; and trough. Most economists agree that the level of business investment, the availability of money and credit, expectations about future economic activity, and other external factors have an impact on the business cycle. Economists analyze leading, coincident, and lagging indicators to determine the occurrence or duration of a particular phase in the business cycle and to predict where the economy is headed.

REVIEW QUESTIONS

1. Define the following terms: business cycle, expansion, peak, contraction, recession, depression, trough, leading indicators, coincident indicators, lagging indicators.

2. Describe the cyclical nature of economic activity.

3. How do supply and demand shape economic activity?

4. How does government policy affect economic activity?

5. **Thinking and Writing Critically**
   In what ways might your expectations about the economy's future influence your current spending habits? Support your explanation.

6. **Applying** Role of Government

   Consult online news sources to investigate what the government has done to affect economic activity. How has it promoted economic expansion and acted to prevent recession? Record your findings and examples.

CHAPTER 10 — ECONOMIC PERFORMANCE

SUMMARY

Economic growth refers to long-term overall improvements in a nation's economy and standard of living. Economic growth is defined as the increase in a nation's real GDP over time. To account for population growth, economists usually measure economic growth in terms of an increase in real GDP per capita. Strong economic growth enables the United States to maintain a high standard of living and compete effectively in global markets.

Achieving economic growth requires an increase either in a nation's inputs—its factors of production—or in the productivity of these inputs. To measure productivity, economists look at labor productivity, or the amount that each worker produces in a given period of time, usually one hour. Productivity growth is defined as an increase in output per worker per hour. The level of available technology, the capital-to-labor ratio, and the education and skill level of the labor force have an impact on productivity growth.

REVIEW QUESTIONS

1. Define the following terms: real GDP per capita, labor productivity, productivity growth, capital-to-labor ratio, capital deepening.

2. How does a society benefit from economic growth?

3. What factors can stimulate the economy?

4. How can productivity be improved?

5. **Thinking and Writing Critically**
   Economists have different points of view about what accounts for the slowing of productivity in the U.S. What are some of their arguments? Which argument do you support and why?

6. **Applying Productivity**
   How does your own productivity allow you to compete in school in terms of grades? What happens to your standing in your class if your productivity falls or rises?

CHAPTER 11 — ECONOMIC CHALLENGES

SUMMARY

Unemployment is an important macroeconomic issue because it hurts the economy as a whole. Economists measure unemployment by identifying the number of employed and the number of unemployed and by determining the unemployment rate. The unemployment rate is the percentage of people in the civilian labor force who do not have jobs but are actively seeking employment. It is not entirely accurate, however, because it does not include the number of people who either lack jobs but have stopped looking for work or who are underemployed.

Four major types of unemployment exist: frictional unemployment, structural unemployment, seasonal unemployment, and cyclical unemployment. Although some frictional and structural unemployment occurs even in a healthy economy, unemployment in general has great economic and social costs.

REVIEW QUESTIONS

1. Define the following terms: unemployment rate, marginally attached workers, discouraged workers, underemployed, frictional unemployment, structural unemployment, seasonal unemployment, cyclical unemployment.

2. What are the shortcomings of the unemployment rate?

3. What is the relationship between employment and product prices, according to some economists?

4. What type of unemployment is considered a healthy part of the economy and why?

5. **Thinking and Writing Critically**

   How does the unemployment rate reflect the state of the economy?

6. **Applying** Unemployment

   Research online news sources to find out how the unemployment rate has changed over the year. Record your findings. What does this tell you about the state of the economy?

CHAPTER 11   **ECONOMIC CHALLENGES**

STUDY GUIDE 11.2

SUMMARY

Economists analyze price fluctuations by examining the price level, inflation, and deflation. The price level influences aggregate supply, or total production throughout the economy, and aggregate demand, or total spending and investment throughout the economy. Inflation is an increase in the average price level of all goods and services in the economy, and deflation is a decrease in the average price level of products. Inflation caused by demand growing faster than supply is known as demand-pull inflation. Inflation caused by rising production costs is known as cost-push inflation.

Economists use both the consumer price index (CPI) and the producer price index (PPI) to measure the amount of price fluctuations. These price indexes estimate the inflation rate, or the pace at which the price level increases. Inflation affects the purchasing power of the dollar, the value of real wages, interest rates, saving and investing, and production costs.

REVIEW QUESTIONS

1. Define the following terms: aggregate supply, aggregate demand, inflation, deflation, demand-pull inflation, cost-push inflation, supply shock, wage-price spiral, consumer price index, market basket, producer price index, inflation rate, hyperinflation.

2. How does price level affect aggregate supply and demand?

3. What rate of inflation do most economists consider to be high?

4. What are the effects of inflation?

5. **Thinking and Writing Critically**
   Suppose that the consumer price index is going to be calculated for your classroom and you are to select the market basket. What products would you put in it? Explain your choices.

6. **Applying** Inflation & Deflation
   Provide a real-life example of a product affected by inflation. By how much did its price change? What do you think caused the price inflation?

CHAPTER 11

ECONOMIC CHALLENGES

STUDY GUIDE 11.3

SUMMARY

Growing income inequality in the United States can be seen in a large gap between the incomes of the rich and the poor. In 1995 some 36.4 million people in the United States lived in poverty.

The Census Bureau classifies people as living in poverty if their total income falls below designated income levels known as the poverty threshold. This threshold is determined largely by the cost of food. The poverty rate is the percentage of people in the total population who are living in poverty.

The Lorenz Curve illustrates how a nation's distribution of income differs from a perfectly proportional distribution of income. The Gini Index provides a statistical measure of income inequality.

Economists believe that the income gap has grown for a variety of reasons. First, the composition of households in the United States has changed. Second, the labor market has changed. Third, technology has caused dramatic shifts in employment and income. Fourth, the growth of a global economy has encouraged many U.S. companies to relocate production to other countries.

REVIEW QUESTIONS

1. Define the following terms: poverty threshold, poverty rate, Lorenz Curve, Gini Index.

2. What is the difference between the poverty threshold and the poverty rate?

3. How do measures of income distribution tend to overemphasize income inequality?

4. To what do economists attribute the widening income gap?

5. **Thinking and Writing Critically**
   What policies or programs do you think would most effectively help close the income gap? Consider the roles of the government, education, and income as potential factors in influencing the size of the income gap. Explain your answer.

6. **Applying** Income Distribution
   What determines the distribution of income? How does demand for a person's skills, talents, and education affect that person's income level?

ROLE OF GOVERNMENT

SUMMARY

In 1994 more than 19 million people worked for the federal, state, and local governments in the United States. Government has not always been a key employer, however; until the late 1800s the government was very small.

Throughout the 1900s all levels of U.S. government have grown in size and complexity because of various factors. These factors include population growth, changing public attitudes, a rising standard of living, and national emergencies.

The introduction of new government programs has increased government spending at the federal, state, and local levels. Education, public welfare, and interest on debts are among the largest expenditures for governments at all levels.

REVIEW QUESTIONS

1. Define the following terms: embargo, per capita.

2. What event changed public opinion about the role of government in economics?

3. In what ways has the U.S. government grown?

4. Which level of government spends the most money, and where is about 50 percent of it spent?

5. **Thinking and Writing Critically**

   What federal assistance programs have expanded with the government? Why have they grown?

6. **Applying** Role of Government

   Conduct research on line to find information about your state government's budget. How is your state's money spent?

CHAPTER 12

ROLE OF GOVERNMENT

STUDY GUIDE 12.2

SUMMARY

In the United States, government has four basic economic goals: to regulate business, provide public goods, promote citizens' economic well-being, and stabilize the economy. The first three goals are shared by the federal, state, and local governments, while the federal government alone works to stabilize the economy.

Government involvement in the U.S. economy has increased dramatically since the abandonment of laissez-faire economic policies in the 1930s. Federal, state, and local governments regulate business to prevent abuses, protect consumers, limit negative externalities, and promote competition.

Governments often share responsibility for providing public goods to their citizens. In some cases, however, privatization has shifted that responsibility from the government to private companies.

The government promotes economic well-being by working to improve the standard of living. In addition, transfer payments allow the government to redistribute wealth.

The federal government acts to stabilize the economy by moderating the business cycle and responding to market failures. These two functions enable the government to minimize the effects of recessions, encourage competition, and promote fair business practices.

REVIEW QUESTIONS

1. Define the following terms: privatization, transfer payment.

2. How does the U.S. government regulate business?

3. How do government regulations protect workers and consumers?

4. What is the government's role in providing public goods?

5. **Thinking and Writing Critically**
   How does the government promote economic well-being in your community? Consider the assistance programs available to people in your area. Explain your answer.

6. **Applying** Role of Government
   Why does the federal government work alone to stabilize the economy? In what ways does it work to achieve economic stabilization? Provide examples.

ROLE OF GOVERNMENT

STUDY GUIDE 12.3

SUMMARY

In the free-enterprise economy of the United States, individuals and groups can influence government economic policies. The government often attempts to introduce programs that serve the public interest. At times, however, these programs may conflict with the desires of individual citizens.

Economic policy and regulations can influence all aspects of production and consumption. In particular, regulations affect prices, services, profits, and productivity. By electing people with economic views similar to their own, citizens can influence economic policy as individuals.

Interest groups also can influence both the election and the policy making of public officials. Their methods include providing information to elected representatives, contributing to campaigns, and encouraging their members to vote for a particular candidate. Many interest groups rely on professional lobbyists to promote their goals.

REVIEW QUESTIONS

1. Define the following terms: interest group, lobbyist.

2. How do the roles of government and citizens interact in upholding the public interest?

3. How do prices, profits, and productivity respond to deregulation?

4. Why does regulation affect production, distribution, and consumption?

5. **Thinking and Writing Critically**
   Describe a situation in which you have attempted to persuade someone, such as a school club or employer, to adopt an action or policy that would benefit you or a group to which you belong. What was the result? Compare your methods to those used by lobbyists or interest groups.

6. **Applying** Role of Government
   Look up information about an interest group in your community on the Internet or at your local library. What are its goals and activities? Summarize your findings.

CHAPTER 13 — MONEY AND THE BANKING SYSTEM

STUDY GUIDE 13.1

SUMMARY

Money is a key to the economic process. For centuries people have traded and bartered, but the use of money has made more sophisticated transactions possible.

Money has three basic functions. As a medium of exchange, money is accepted in exchange for products. As a standard of value, money provides a basis for price comparison. As a store of value, money can be saved for later use.

Money has five major characteristics: durability, portability, divisibility, stability in value, and acceptability. Durability means that money can be used repeatedly, and portability means that money is easy to move. Divisibility allows money to be divided into smaller units. Stability in value means that money retains its value over time, and acceptability means that people recognize and accept money in exchange for goods and services.

Societies use different items as money. Some societies rely on commodity money, while others use representative money and fiat money. The United States relies on fiat money in the form of coins, paper money, checks, and near money.

REVIEW QUESTIONS

1. Define the following terms: medium of exchange, standard of value, commodity money, representative money, specie, fiat money, currency, near money.

2. Why is money's function as a standard of value important?

3. Why does money assist in the exchange of goods?

4. What differentiates fiat money from representative money?

5. **Thinking and Writing Critically**
   What do you think would happen to the global economy if money was not widely accepted? Consider the money tourism earns and how people use money daily.

6. **Applying** Exchange, Money, & Interdependence
   What types of currency exist around the world? Using the Internet, identify the currencies of five foreign countries. What are they called? How does the value of each currency compare to that of the U.S. dollar? List your results.

CHAPTER 13 — MONEY AND THE BANKING SYSTEM

SUMMARY

Like money, banking has evolved to meet the needs of a changing U.S. society. Throughout much of U.S. history, the idea of a central bank has been controversial. In the late 1700s the federal government established the Bank of the United States, which operated from 1791 to 1811. The Second Bank of the United States operated from 1816 to 1836.

Problems with the First and Second Banks led to a period of unregulated state banking. Financial panics and the Civil War, however, persuaded Congress to establish a national banking system.

Further troubles and panics led to the development of the Federal Reserve System and the era of modern banking. Under President Franklin D. Roosevelt, economic reforms gave the federal government a larger role in the banking system.

Banking services expanded during the 1960s and 1970s as banks began to extend more loans to individuals. Additionally, some people felt that their needs were not met by traditional banking practices, and opened specialized banks.

REVIEW QUESTIONS

1. Define gold standard.

2. What goals did the First Bank of the United States accomplish?

3. What problems were associated with the banking system that was established after the Civil War?

4. What did the post-World War II banking system set out to do?

5. **Thinking and Writing Critically**
   What led to the loss of public confidence in the first three U.S. banking systems? How has the government worked to restore public confidence since then?

6. **Applying** Economic Institutions & Incentives
   Why did the government buy all the gold held by U.S. banks? How did it change how money was valued? What other countries have eliminated the gold standard? Conduct an Internet search to help you find out.

CHAPTER 13 — MONEY AND THE BANKING SYSTEM

STUDY GUIDE 13.3

SUMMARY

Americans' banking choices broadened to include a wide variety of financial institutions: commercial banks, savings and loan associations, mutual savings banks, and credit unions. Technological advances have led to automated banking. Federal deregulation has led to competition and reorganization in the banking industry. Additionally, poor lending practices and uncertain insurance programs contributed to the collapse of many financial institutions in the 1980s. By the 1990s the U.S. government had stabilized the banking industry and resolved—often at taxpayer expense—many of the problems that had caused the crisis.

REVIEW QUESTIONS

1. Define the following terms: commercial banks, savings and loan associations, mutual savings banks, debit card, deregulation, default.

2. What three trends have emerged in banking?

3. What services do the four types of financial institutions have in common?

4. How has deregulation increased competition in banking?

5. Thinking and Writing Critically

How can loan defaults contribute to bank failures? Provide an example to support your answer.

6. Applying Economic Institutions & Incentives

How is it possible to conduct your banking needs without stepping into a bank? Explain your answer.

THE FEDERAL RESERVE AND MONETARY POLICY

CHAPTER 14

STUDY GUIDE 14.1

SUMMARY

Before 1913 central banking had a stormy history in the United States. Repeated panic runs—notably the Panic of 1907—and other banking problems led to the creation of the Federal Reserve system in 1913.

The Federal Reserve system, or the "Fed," acts as the central bank of the United States. The Fed provides commercial banks and the government a reliable source of cash, holds ready cash reserves to be used for short-term borrowing by these institutions, and makes large loans to these institutions to stabilize the national monetary and banking systems.

Several features distinguish the Fed from central banks in other countries. These include the lack of a single central bank, ownership and control by the member banks, and nonmandatory membership for some banks.

The Fed is organized on district and national levels, and is composed of 12 district Federal Reserve banks. The actions of these district banks are coordinated by a central decision-making authority in Washington, D.C., called the Board of Governors.

REVIEW QUESTIONS

1. Define pyramided reserves.

2. Why was the Federal Reserve created?

3. What are the responsibilities of the Fed?

4. How is the Fed prevented from gaining too much power over the nation's economy?

5. **Thinking and Writing Critically**
    Explain why the Panic of 1907 changed citizens' attitudes toward a central banking system. How did public opinion change?

6. **Applying** Economic Institutions & Incentives
    Search current new sources to find out more about the Fed. What decisions has the Fed made lately? How have the Fed's decisions affected the national economy?

CHAPTER 14

THE FEDERAL RESERVE AND MONETARY POLICY

STUDY GUIDE 14.2

SUMMARY

The Federal Reserve System provides a number of banking services in the U.S. economy. The activities of the Federal Reserve can be divided into two categories: services to banks and services to the government.

The Fed oversees the flow of money among member banks and its district banks, mainly by clearing checks and by making loans to commercial banks. The Fed manages the U.S. government's financial activities by serving as the government's bank, supervising member banks, and regulating the money supply.

Economists measure the money supply in different ways. These measures are known as M1, M2, and M3. M1 includes the most limited amount of funds, while M3 includes the widest amount. Each type is distinguished by how it identifies "readily available" money.

REVIEW QUESTIONS

1. Define the following terms: check clearing, money supply.

2. Why are the Fed's services to banks an indirect service to consumers?

3. How are the government's financial activities managed?

4. How the measurements of U.S. money supply classified?

5. **Thinking and Writing Critically**
   Imagine you just wrote a $30 check to the phone company to pay your bill. What process does the check go through to be cleared? Explain your answer.

6. **Applying** Economic Exchange, Money, & Independence

   Suppose you have a worn out $20 bill. What happens to that bill when your local bank receives it?

CHAPTER 14

THE FEDERAL RESERVE AND MONETARY POLICY

STUDY GUIDE 14.3

SUMMARY

Through its monetary policy, the Fed attempts to promote economic growth and stability as well as to avoid recessions. To reach these goals, the Fed pursues either an easy-money policy or a tight-money policy. An easy-money policy is characterized by low interest rates and is used in times of recession to expand the money supply, increase aggregate demand, create jobs and reduce unemployment, and promote economic growth. A tight-money policy is characterized by higher interest rates and a contracting money supply. It is used during periods of inflation to slow business activity and stabilize prices.

The Fed's three major tools of monetary policy are open-market operations, the discount rate, and reserve requirements. Other policy tools include margin requirements, credit regulation, and moral suasion. The Fed's actions, however, are limited by several factors, including economic forecasts, time lags in developing and carrying out monetary policy, priorities and trade-offs, lack of coordination among government agencies in forming economic policies, and conflicting opinions about monetary policy.

REVIEW QUESTIONS

1. Define the following terms: monetary policy, easy-money policy, tight-money policy, discount rate, prime rate, reserve requirement, margin requirement, moral suasion.

2. What are the goals of monetary policy?

3. How does the Fed determine whether to adopt an easy-money or tight-money policy?

4. What indirect controls does the Fed use to influence aggregate demand in the economy?

5. **Thinking and Writing Critically**
Describe a time when you had to carry out a particular job at school or at work. Think about the Fed's main challenges in completing its job. How have you experienced similar obstacles? Explain your answer.

6. **Applying** Economic Institutions & Incentives
Using the Internet, research a topic such as easy-money and tight-money policies, the reserve requirement, the discount rate, or the prime rate to learn how they apply in the world. Summarize what you have discovered.

FISCAL POLICY

STUDY GUIDE 15.1

SUMMARY

In addition to monetary policy, the government uses fiscal policy to influence the economy. Fiscal policy is the use of government income and expenditures to manage the economy.

Federal, state, and local governments in the United States must finance their operations through various kinds of taxes. The federal government raises most of its revenues through individual income taxes, corporate income taxes, and Social Security taxes. Excise taxes, estate taxes, gift taxes, and customs duties make up a much smaller portion of federal taxes. State and local governments raise revenues primarily through individual income taxes, sales taxes, and property taxes.

REVIEW QUESTIONS

1. Define the following terms: fiscal policy, tax rate, excise tax, estate tax, gift tax, customs duty.

2. How does the government use taxes in fiscal policy?

3. How do different tax rates affect taxpayers?

4. What kinds of taxes supply the government with the most revenue?

5. Thinking and Writing Critically

Of these items: eggs, jewelry, and milk, which are subject to sales tax and which are exempt? How is sales tax an example of a regressive tax? Explain your answer.

6. Applying Fiscal Policy

Why is property tax a controversial subject? Research news sources to find examples to support your answer.

CHAPTER 15

FISCAL POLICY

STUDY GUIDE 15.2

SUMMARY

Fiscal policy is influenced by the schools of supply-side economics and demand-side economics, both of which pursue the goal of economic growth. During the 1980s, supply-side economics influenced public economic policy in the United States. Supply-side economics concentrates on increasing the nation's aggregate supply. The federal government has often used fiscal policy based upon the demand-side theories of John Maynard Keynes to regulate aggregate demand and promote economic growth and stability in the economy.

The chief tools of fiscal policy are marginal tax rates, tax incentives, government spending, public transfer payments, and the progressive income tax. Fiscal planners use these tools whether they believe in supply-side theory or demand-side theory.

Fiscal policy has several limitations. Timing problems often occur because there are delays in putting policy into effect. Political pressures arise because fiscal policy is developed by elected officials. These officials often are reluctant to introduce unpopular policies such as tax increases and cuts to popular programs. Policies sometimes create undesired effects because economic behavior is often unpredictable. Finally, agencies within the federal government do not always coordinate federal fiscal policies. In addition, state and local governments often have policies that differ from the federal government's fiscal policy.

REVIEW QUESTIONS

1. Define the following terms: supply-side economics, demand-side economics, tax incentive, restrictive fiscal policy, expansionary fiscal policy.

2. What effects do supply-side economics and demand-side economics have on fiscal policy?

3. Under what circumstances does the government change fiscal policy?

4. What are the challenges facing the enactment of fiscal policy?

5. **Thinking and Writing Critically**
   What are the criticisms of supply-side economics? Do you agree or disagree with critics of this economic theory? Which economic theory do you support, demand-side or supply-side economics? Why? Explain your response.

6. **Applying** Fiscal Policy
   Conduct an Internet search to discover fiscal policy strategies supported by members of your state congress or of the U.S. Congress. What strategies are supported and by which senators and representatives?

CHAPTER 15

FISCAL POLICY

STUDY GUIDE 15.3

SUMMARY

Currently, all governments develop budgets to help them plan revenues and the amounts and direction of expenditures. The federal government has full-time executive and legislative offices that work only on the budget.

The budget is developed by the president, in consultation with advisers. This proposal is then analyzed by both houses of Congress. When both houses have approved the budget, it is returned to the president for signing. The president may veto the budget, however, if congressional changes are not acceptable.

Federal spending in particular has grown significantly. Deficit spending since World War II has caused great increases in annual budget deficits. Some citizens and policy makers believe that an amendment should be added to the U.S. Constitution requiring the federal government to have a balanced budget.

REVIEW QUESTIONS

1. Define the following terms: federal budget, fiscal year, budget deficit, deficit spending, national debt, debt ceiling.

2. What is the relationship between the federal budget and fiscal policy?

3. Why was a federal budget established and by what process is it created?

4. Why is it important to balance the budget?

5. **Thinking and Writing Critically**

   What are the opinions of economists about the impact of the national debt on the economy? Which argument do you support? Explain your answer.

6. **Applying** Role of Government

   Investigate the current state of the federal budget from an Internet search of news sources. Record your findings.

CHAPTER 16 · COMPARING ECONOMIC SYSTEMS

SUMMARY

Economic systems can be classified by ownership of capital and by the process of answering the questions of what, how, and for whom to produce. The four kinds of economic systems arising from this classification are market capitalism, command capitalism, market socialism, and communism. In a market capitalist system, capital is privately owned, and decisions are made primarily by the owners of capital. In a command capitalist system, economic decisions are frequently made by the government. In a market socialist system, capital is generally owned by the government, which makes many economic decisions, although individuals and businesses also have important decision-making roles. In a communist system, nearly all capital is owned—and nearly all decisions are made—by the government.

REVIEW QUESTIONS

1. Define the following terms: market system, command system, market socialism.

2. How are economic systems determined?

3. Which economic systems are controlled by government, and which are controlled by individuals and enterprises?

4. What role does government have in market capitalism?

5. Thinking and Writing Critically

Why is socialism thought to have failed in some countries recently? Explain your answer.

6. Applying Economic Systems

If your school were an economic system, what type would it be? Consider who decides what, how, and for whom to produce, what capital is available, and who owns it.

CHAPTER 16 — COMPARING ECONOMIC SYSTEMS

STUDY GUIDE 16.2

SUMMARY

Capitalism emerged in Europe during the 1700s and 1800s, as nations moved away from mercantilism and governments became less involved in economic decision making. One of the major economic thinkers of the day was Adam Smith, who argued that a market economy was largely self-regulating and did not require government involvement.

Forms of capitalism vary widely around the world. While the United States and Germany are market capitalist systems with relatively limited government involvement, other nations such as Japan follow command capitalism.

REVIEW QUESTIONS

1. Define the following terms: mercantilism, indicative planning, nationalization.

2. Why did capitalism emerge as the dominant economic system in the 1800s?

3. Why is France's economic system not a command capitalist system?

4. How have the economies of Japan and South Korea used incentives to encourage the growth of their economies?

5. **Thinking and Writing Critically**
   How did Germany's economic system change after World War II? Explain your answer.

6. **Applying** Economic Systems
   Use the Internet to learn what other countries around the world have capitalist economies. List three of them. Has each nation always had a free-enterprise system? When did it convert to capitalism? Record your findings.

CHAPTER 16 — COMPARING ECONOMIC SYSTEMS

SUMMARY

Socialism arose from dissatisfaction with working and living conditions during the early Industrial Revolution. Early socialist thinkers such as Robert Owen and Charles Fourier sought a more equal distribution of wealth.

Market socialism, also called democratic socialism, is characterized by the people having basic human rights and electing government officials, which gives them some control over their country's economic planning. This system was seen in Sweden, where the government owned some of the country's industries.

REVIEW QUESTIONS

1. What is the basis of socialism?

2. What are the goals of central planning?

3. What was the response to harsh working conditions and a decline in workers' quality of life during the Industrial Revolution?

4. How was Sweden economic system a model of market socialism?

5. Thinking and Writing Critically

Explain the relationship between economic socialism and political freedom. Are they interdependent or independent of each other? Provide examples to support your answer.

6. Applying Economic Systems

During the 1800s, many utopias, or communities designed to create the ideal society, were established in the U.S. Does market socialism seem to be a good basis for an ideal society? Explain your answer.

CHAPTER 16

COMPARING ECONOMIC SYSTEMS

STUDY GUIDE 16.4

SUMMARY

Command socialism, also called authoritarian socialism or communism, developed primarily from the views of German philosopher Karl Marx. He believed that history was a series of class struggles that would eventually result in collective ownership of all capital.

The Soviet Union was the most influential nation to rely on communism. The leaders of the Soviet Union abolished private property, redistributed land, and developed a rigidly centralized economy. By the 1980s, poor economic performance led to a call for reforms. In 1991 the Soviet Union collapsed.

The communist People's Republic of China has moved from strict communism to a more market-oriented form of socialism. For many years, China relied on central planning, but low productivity led to economic turmoil. Market reforms have encouraged many in China to call for political reforms, and economic growth has raised China's standard of living.

REVIEW QUESTIONS

1. Define the following terms: bourgeoisie, proletariat, collectivization, perestroika, household responsibility system.

2. What model of socialism does communism represent?

3. What led to the collapse of communism in the former Soviet Union?

4. How did China move toward more market-responsive policies, and what were some associated reforms?

5. **Thinking and Writing Critically**
   What made up the foundation of Karl Marx's theories? What were some of the problems with his assumptions?

6. **Applying** Economic Institutions & Incentives
   Why did a lack of incentives contribute to the shortcomings of communism? Explain your answer.

CHAPTER 17

DEVELOPING COUNTRIES

STUDY GUIDE 17.1

SUMMARY

Of the nearly 200 countries in the world today, some 25 are classified as developed nations. The others are known as developing nations. Developing nations generally share such characteristics as low per capita GNI, limited resources, rapid population growth rates, and traditional agricultural or one-crop economies.

The lowest-income developing nations have per capita GNI of $700 or less. Other developing nations have per capita GNI of between $701 and $12,000, while developed nations have per capita GNI of $12,001 or more.

Resource limitations in developing nations stem from limited natural resources, such as a lack of arable land, and historic forces, such as European colonization. The inefficient use of resources in developing nations also can hinder economic development.

Population growth in developing nations is much higher than that in developed nations. In fact, developing nations have population-growth rates that are about three times those of developed nations. As a result, most population growth between 1990 and 2000 is expected to have taken place in developing nations.

Most people in developing nations depend on subsistence agriculture, growing just enough to meet basic needs. Some developing nations have been able to produce surpluses in the form of commercial plantation crops. Profits from these crops are most likely to benefit the producers, who tend to be wealthy landowners, rather than the country's general population.

REVIEW QUESTIONS

1. Define the following terms: economic development, arable, subsistence agriculture.

2. How do developing and developed nations differ?

3. How does the World Bank determine the economic ranking of nations?

4. What characterizes traditional agricultural economies?

5. **Thinking and Writing Critically**
   How is population growth explained? What explanations do experts have to account for population growth?

6. **Applying** International Growth & Stability
   Research online news sources to find an example of a developing nation whose economy has been affected by government or business policy. Identify the policy affecting the nation and explain its effect on the country's economy.

CHAPTER 17

DEVELOPING COUNTRIES

STUDY GUIDE 17.2

SUMMARY

Developing nations experience scarcity and underutilization of resources. The scarcity and misuse of the factors of production—land, labor, capital, and entrepreneurship—restricts economic growth.

Other obstacles to economic development include an inadequate infrastructure, political instability, and social and cultural issues. A nation that lacks a well-built road system, for example, is likely to have difficulty maintaining reliable markets. Political struggles can disrupt business activity and destroy capital resources, and social and cultural issues may make people reluctant to change traditional methods of production and exchange.

REVIEW QUESTIONS

1. Define the following terms: one-crop economy, capital formation, expropriation.

2. Why do many developing nations experience slow economic growth?

3. What can limit the productivity of workers in developing nations?

4. For what reasons are many investors reluctant to invest in the economies of developing nations?

5. **Thinking and Writing Critically**
   Consider the many challenges developing nations face to increase economic growth. Suggest ways a developing nation might be able overcome these obstacles.

6. **Applying** Scarcity & Choice
   What effect does subsistence have on the economic growth of developing nations?

CHAPTER 17 — DEVELOPING COUNTRIES

SUMMARY

Leaders of developing nations use either a socialist or a capitalist model of decision making. Regardless of which model the leaders use, however, they must establish development plans to guide the use of their scarce resources. In creating these plans, leaders must consider all the production possibilities and trade-offs related to a proposed course of action.

Developing nations rely on both domestic and foreign funds to finance economic development. Domestic savings is an important source of funds in many nations, but most seek foreign capital as well. Banks, multinational corporations, and nonprofit organizations supply vast amounts of private capital for development. Money and training from foreign governments and international organizations are also crucial to economic development.

REVIEW QUESTIONS

1. Define the following terms: land reform, multinational corporation.

2. How are decisions made differently in the socialist and capitalist models?

3. Through what means can developing nations expand their production possibilities?

4. How do developing nations obtain financial help in the global community?

5. **Thinking and Writing Critically**
   Why do experts question the effectiveness of foreign aid? What do they suggest will improve effectiveness? What is often the response from recipients of foreign aid? Which point of view do you support and why?

6. **Applying Trade-Offs & Opportunity Costs**
   Why would a developing nation need to make trade-offs because of the problem of scarcity? What kinds of trade-offs might a developing nation need to make?

CHAPTER 18

INTERNATIONAL TRADE

SUMMARY

International trade has two important characteristics. First, it is voluntary. Second, it creates wealth. International trade encourages individuals and businesses to specialize—to produce a limited number of goods and services. This specialization leads to worldwide interdependence. Specialization often occurs because a nation has certain human or natural resources that other nations do not.

How a nation decides what to produce is determined by absolute and comparative advantage—two related economic concepts originally described by economist David Ricardo in the 1800s. A nation has an absolute advantage in producing a certain good when it can do so with greater efficiency than can its trading partner. A nation's comparative advantage is determined by calculating where the largest absolute advantage occurs for each good.

REVIEW QUESTIONS

1. Define the following terms: absolute advantage, comparative advantage.

2. Why does international trade benefit participating nations?

3. What advantage does specialization offer a country?

4. How do comparative advantage and specialization relate?

5. **Thinking and Writing Critically**
   Imagine that you must decide for a nation which products to export. What would you consider in making your decision? Explain your answer.

6. **Applying** Trade-offs & Opportunity Costs
   How do trade-offs apply to the concepts of absolute advantage and comparative advantage? Support your answer.

CHAPTER 18 — INTERNATIONAL TRADE

SUMMARY

The money needed to carry on international trade relies on foreign exchange markets that convert one nation's currency into another's. Once the value of one currency is established in relation to another, a foreign exchange rate has been established.

Since World War II, trading nations have used two foreign exchange systems: first, the adjustable-peg system—introduced at the Bretton Woods Conference in 1944—and later the floating, or flexible, system—established in 1971. The floating exchange rate allows the value of a currency to be determined by the laws of demand and supply and to change from one minute to the next.

Nations determine the strength of their international trade by measuring their balance of payments and balance of trade. Balance of payments is an annual accounting of transactions, and a balance of trade is a record of imports and exports.

REVIEW QUESTIONS

1. Define the following terms: foreign exchange market, foreign exchange rate, adjustable-peg system, devaluation, appreciation, floating exchange rate, balance of payments, balance of trade, trade surplus, trade deficit.

2. Why are foreign exchange markets important?

3. Why was the adjustable-peg system eliminated?

4. How is the balance of payments divided and why?

5. **Thinking and Writing Critically**
   How do interest rates affect the flow of foreign money invested in the U.S.?

6. **Applying** Exchange, Money, & Interdependence
   If you were traveling to another country, how would you determine the value of the U.S. dollar in foreign currency? How quickly could you expect the value to change?

CHAPTER 18

INTERNATIONAL TRADE

STUDY GUIDE 18.3

SUMMARY

Economic and political factors sometimes lead nations to restrict international trade. Common trade barriers include tariffs, import quotas, voluntary trade restrictions, and embargoes.

Nations are said to conduct free trade when international trade is not restricted by governments. Trade barriers sometimes are used to protect domestic industries. Arguments for both free trade and protectionism are based on infant industries, job protection, standard of living, specialization, national security, and fairness.

In recent years, many nations have reduced trade barriers to increase international cooperation. Reciprocal trade agreements impose lower tariffs on goods imported from nations that also reduce tariffs. Regional trade organizations are alliances based on the reduction of trade barriers between members of the alliance. Important examples of international cooperation include the World Trade Organization (WTO) and the North American Free Trade Agreement (NAFTA).

Multinational corporations also increase international trade. Additionally, international joint ventures encourage cooperation among companies in different countries.

REVIEW QUESTIONS

1. Define the following terms: trade barrier, revenue tariff, protective tariff, import quota, voluntary trade restriction, embargo, free trade, protectionism.

2. How does government regulate international trade?

3. For what purposes has the government enacted most embargoes?

4. What is the goal of international cooperation among trading nations?

5. **Thinking and Writing Critically**

   Why do some people support protectionism over free trade? Do you support a protectionism? Explain your point of view.

6. **Applying** International Trade

   Why have multinational corporations that trade with the U.S. opened businesses in the U.S.? How does the U.S. benefit from these new businesses? What new trade issues have resulted?

CHAPTER 1

Section 1.1

1. Refer to the glossary.
2. By examining their economic choices, people can take advantage of opportunities available to them.
3. natural resources, people, manufactured materials and goods, technology, and entrepreneurship
4. Consumers buy what producers make and producers make what consumers want and need.
5. Answers may vary but should indicate a specific business or product and identify potential risks in starting the business or making the product, such as limited resources, costs of technology or resources, and lack of consumer interest or demand.
6. It improves production methods, provides new products, and enhances existing ones. Answers may vary but should specify the product and technology.

Section 1.2

1. Refer to the glossary.
2. forces people to make decisions about how to use resources effectively
3. what to produce, how to produce, and for whom to produce
4. division of labor and specialization
5. Answers may vary but should identify how students were forced to make an economic decision as a result of limited resources, for example being unable to buy all the goods they wanted.
6. Responses may vary but should show an understanding of division of labor, specialization, and productivity.

Section 1.3

1. Refer to the glossary.
2. As economic resources become more available or limited, production possibilities change.
3. trade-offs and opportunity costs
4. because it is based on current assumptions relating to current conditions
5. Answers may vary but should identify a trade-off made, the opportunity cost, and reasons for the decision.
6. Students should indicate that a production possibilities curve should be drawn. Assumptions are that available resources and technology will not change and all resources are being used efficiently. Proposals may vary but should indicate what the company should focus on building.

Section 1.4

1. Refer to the glossary.
2. if they are producing goods efficiently and quickly enough
3. utility and scarcity; allows producers and consumers to decide the relative worth of goods and services in an exchange
4. reduces self-sufficiency and promotes interdependence
5. Answers may vary but should illustrate an understanding of the different forms of exchange. Opinions should be based the advantages and disadvantages of the exchange students think is the most efficient.

6. Students should argue one point of view and use reasoning to support their answers. For example, the Internet may ease the exchange process by making it easier for consumers to buy. On the other hand, it may make it more difficult because of limited payment methods in purchasing items.

CHAPTER 2

Section 2.1

1. Refer to the glossary.
2. reflects the process a nation follows to produce products and helps a nation answer the three basic economic questions
3. traditional, command, market, and mixed; mixed
4. People are motivated to fulfill their own wants and needs, which in turn helps the economy grow.
5. Answers may vary but opinions should demonstrate reasoning and an understanding of the different types of economic systems and their function.
6. Responses may vary but should indicate knowledge of the purpose of incentives and describe a relevant event in which students were given incentives and the effect.

Section 2.2

1. Refer to the glossary.
2. based on the freedom of individuals to make choices without much government intervention
3. producers—provide goods and services in the market; consumers—influence production by purchasing goods and services; and the govern-

ment—oversees and regulates effects of the economic decisions made by producers and consumers

4. how resources, products, and payments are exchanged in the U.S. free-enterprise system

5. Individuals have the right to own private property and contracts, make individual choices, compete in the economy, make decisions based on self-interest, and conduct business with limited government intervention. Examples may vary but should be relevant to the exercise.

6. product—consumers must buy software and a connection to access the Internet; promoter—producers and consumers can buy products over the Internet; examples may vary

Section 2.3

1. Refer to the glossary.

2. to help policymakers choose how to use scarce resources

3. economic freedom: freedom of choice in the marketplace; efficiency: make the best use of economic resources; equity: measurement of fairness in available choices; security: protection from poverty and business failures; stability: achieving full employment and stable prices; and growth: increasing the amount of goods and services each worker produces

4. trade-offs and conflict

5. Answers may vary but should indicate an understanding of the importance of prioritizing goals and provide personal examples.

6. Students should provide concrete examples of the U.S.'s six economic goals and indicate which goals are current priorities.

CHAPTER 3

Section 3.1

1. Refer to the glossary.

2. An increase in price decreases the quantity demanded, and a decrease in price increases the quantity demanded.

3. They sometimes do not apply in affecting the law of demand.

4. They both demonstrate the relationship between product price and quantity demanded.

5. Examples may vary but should indicate which concept they applied in making the choice—income effect, the substitution effect, or diminishing marginal utility.

6. Pricing will indicate whether or not the product is in high or low demand.

Section 3.2

1. Refer to the glossary.

2. number of consumers, decisions made by businesses, policy decisions made by governments, and technology

3. As people's income increases, spending tends to increase, which raises product demand. A drop in people's income has the opposite effect.

4. Because consumers spend based on their anticipated income, their spending, or demand, will change as their expectations change.

5. Examples may vary, but one example should be of a substitute good and one of a complementary good. Students should discuss what influenced their purchasing decisions, for example, price in the case of substitute goods and necessity in the case of complementary goods.

6. Answers may vary, but students should reflect an understanding of the determinants of demand and how they can shift the demand curve.

Section 3.3

1. Refer to the glossary.

2. by determining elasticity of demand based on the total-revenue test

3. whether or not a product is a necessity, whether or not substitutes are available, or whether or not a product's cost represents a large portion of consumers' income

4. A small price increase causes a significant decrease in demand.

5. Answers should be based quantity demanded, total revenue, or elasticity of demand.

6. Example may vary, but students should offer two examples each of an elastic demand (cookies, pizza, and music CDs) and an inelastic demand (electricity, salt, and flour). They should also explain why the examples fall into each category, based on whether a product is or is not a necessity, whether or not substitutes are available, or whether or not a product's cost represents a large portion of consumers' income.

CHAPTER 4

Section 4.1

1. Refer to the glossary.

2. profit

3. supply schedules and supply curves

4. When a small change in a product's price causes a major change in the quantity supplied, supply for the good is elastic. Inelastic supply occurs when a change in a product's price has little impact on the quantity supplied.

5. Answers may vary but should reflect an understanding of the laws of supply and demand and how it affects pricing.

6. If the product can be made quickly, inexpensively, and using a few, readily available resources, it is a elastic supply. Examples include t-shirts, books, and inexpensive toys. If producing it requires a great deal of time, money, and resources that are not readily available, then it is an inelastic supply. Examples include jewelry, leather, and skyscrapers.

Section 4.2
1. Refer to the glossary.
2. The determinants of supply are prices of resources, government tools, technology, competition, prices of related goods, and producer expectations.
3. A drop causes an increase in supply. A rise causes a decrease in supply.
4. Taxes increases cause a decrease in supply and tax reductions causes an increase in supply. Subsidies increase supply. Regulations increase supply when they are lenient and decrease supply when they are strict.
5. Example of businesses may vary. Students should indicate that high competition tends to increase supply and the product prices vary at every level. If demand drops, then businesses might not be able to sell the products in excess supply and therefore might not be able to make enough profit. If this happens, businesses might close.
6. Example may vary. Students might indicate that new technology usually improves production efficiency and lowers production costs.

Section 4.3
1. Refer to the glossary.
2. the need to maximize productivity and by the costs of production
3. look at total product, marginal product, and the law of diminishing returns
4. input—resources used in making products; output—products made
5. If you increase the amount of beef, the output of stew increases. However, increasing the amount of salt does not increase output and, in fact, may make the stew inedible.
6. Students' answers will vary but should consider the costs of food and equipment and how demand might vary at breakfast, lunch, and dinner.

CHAPTER 5
Section 5.1
1. Refer to the glossary.
2. because they are the main form of communication between producers and consumers in a free-enterprise market
3. Producers communicate the production and distribution costs of goods and services to consumers. By rejecting or accepting the price, consumers communicate whether or not an established price is acceptable.
4. Flexibility adapts to changes in supply and demand of goods, but it can lead to instability in the marketplace.
5. Answers may vary but should refer to one of the benefits of the price system. For example, choice might allow students to compare products and prices, allowing them to buy the best product and the best cost.
6. Prices for the damaged crops would rise because supply would be scarce. This reaction represents a benefit because it helps prevent demand from surpassing supply.

Section 5.2
1. Refer to the glossary.
2. the price system
3. shifts in supply and demand
4. surplus—lower price to try to increase profits; shortage—raise price to reduce demand; trial and error
5. Answers may vary but might discuss how consumer tastes, market size, or competition might affect sales and how pricing may be determined by inventory surplus and shortages or competition.
6. September—supply increases, equilibrium point shifts down and to the right; October—supply and demand increase, equilibrium point shifts right; November—supply and demand decline, equilibrium point shifts left

Section 5.3
1. Refer to the glossary.
2. set prices or ration goods
3. It interferes with the normal interaction of supply and demand and can maintain or worsen market imbalances.
4. price ceiling—rent control; price floor—minimum wage
5. They say it is unfair and that a price system remains neutral; it is expensive to put into effect, while a price system costs nothing to administer; and it creates a black market, which is another unfair system. Arguments for or against rationing should display reasoning.

6. Responses may vary but should reflect an understanding of price floors. Students might respond that income could be positively or negatively affected depending on the demand for and the value of the job they are doing. They might respond to any changes in income by working more hours, spending less money, or finding another job.

CHAPTER 6
Section 6.1
1. Refer to the glossary.
2. encourages producers to supply consumers with a wide selection of goods and services that are priced fairly
3. It is necessary for buyers to make informed purchasing decisions and sellers to be able enter or exit a market easily.
4. Buyers and sellers compete under the laws of supply and demand and must act independently. Buyers need to be well-informed about products, and sellers must have ease of market entry or exit.
5. Answers may vary but should indicate an understanding of product differentiation, perfect competition, and monopolistic competition.
6. Answers will vary but should reflect an understanding of monopolistic competition and perfect competition.

Section 6.2
1. Refer to the glossary.
2. higher prices, fewer sellers, and fewer products from which to choose
3. control prices through non-price competition, independent pricing, collusion, and cartels

4. The size of the seller might allow it use its resources more efficiently than its competition. Geographic location may be so limited that only one seller enters the market. A seller might advance technologically over its competitors, allowing it improve production of an existing product. When products cannot be sold effectively through the price system, government is the sole seller of products.
5. If monopolies raise prices too high, they can attract competitors and decrease demand. Cartels protect sellers' market shares.
6. Responses may vary but should indicate an understanding of what defines a monopoly and how monopolies can form. For example, a cable company could be an example of a seller that started out as a monopoly because of the size of its resources. General Electric could be an example of a company that established a monopoly over Trident submarines because it developed patented technology in making that type of submarine.

Section 6.3
1. Refer to the glossary.
2. growing concern over the amount of control trusts had over the marketplace and to protect consumers and ensure market competition
3. passed several antitrust laws
4. through the Federal Trade Commission
5. Responses may vary but students should recognize a monopoly exists when only one seller provides products at the school.

6. Responses may vary but should reflect an understanding of how antitrust legislation protects consumers from unfair business practices, such as price setting and price discrimination.

CHAPTER 7
Section 7.1
1. Refer to the glossary.
2. They require small amounts of money to start up and run. Also, the business has full control of operations and all rights to profits.
3. lawyers, plumbers, carpenters, hairstylists, florists, and farmers
4. Because business owners are personally responsible for business debts (unlimited liability), a business may close to make debt payments. Because business owners are responsible for all aspects of running the business (sole responsibility), their sense of satisfaction and accomplishment could be reduced. Having limited collateral, owners may not receive financial capital from a lender to expand the business (limited growth potential). Because sole proprietorships depend on one person, risk of failure is greater (lack of longevity).
5. Responses may vary. Advantages might include complete control over the business (homework and studying) and exclusive right to profit (good grades). Disadvantages might include sole responsibility for performing required work and getting good grades.
6. Responses may vary but should reflect an understanding of the characteristics of a sole proprietorship.

Section 7.2

1. Refer to the glossary.
2. specialization and shared responsibility, shared decision-making, and shared business losses
3. They are easy to set up, have unlimited liability, and have a lack of longevity.
4. In a general partnership, partners share making decisions and are active in the business. In a limited partnership, partners have an inactive role in the business, share profits, and have limited liability.
5. Answers may vary. Students might indicate that working alone would allow them to control the work, avoid conflict, and have exclusive right to the grade. On the other hand, they might choose to work as a group because the workload and decision making would be shared.
6. Answers may vary but should indicate an understanding of the benefits and liabilities of general and limited partnerships.

Section 7.3

1. Refer to the glossary.
2. treated as individuals and legally distinct from their owners
3. submit articles of incorporation and receive corporate charter, which is approved by state officials
4. can receive dividends, limited liability, flexibility in buying and selling shares, and earn money without working for it
5. board of directors—school board; officers—administration and teachers; shareholders—parents and students; and dividends—education
6. Examples may vary. Students should find an example of a

decision made by a company's board of directors using current online news sources and demonstrate understanding of the different type of decisions a board can make, such as decisions about policy, corporate development, selecting new officers, and fundraising.

Section 7.4

1. Refer to the glossary.
2. merging horizontally, vertically, or into a conglomerate
3. advantages—company increases efficiency, lowers costs, and increases size; disadvantages—higher rates of unemployment and risks of reduced competition may lead to higher prices for consumers
4. purchasing cooperatives—retail stores that buy large amounts of merchandise at reduced prices and pass savings on to members; marketing cooperatives—established by farmers who hope to secure higher process for their products; service cooperatives—provide members with services, like utilities, health care, and legal assistance; and financial cooperatives—lend members money at reduced interest rates
5. Answers may vary but students might respond that if they want to buy some of the competition, a horizontal merger would be best. If they want to expand to control more phases of production, then a vertical combination would be best.
6. Examples may vary but should reflect an understanding of the different organizations listed.

CHAPTER 8
Section 8.1

1. Refer to the glossary.
2. all people who are at least 16 years old and who are working or looking for work
3. If an occupation has several potential workers (supply) but few available jobs (demand), then wages tend to be low. If an occupation has few potential workers (supply) but many available jobs (demand), then wages tend to be high.
4. passed antidiscrimination and minimum-wage laws, such as the Civil Rights Act of 1964 and the Fair Labor Standards.
5. Answers may vary but should indicate that people have become more educated and more skilled. Also, more jobs have become available with advances in technology.
6. Students should find that as educational experience increases, salary tends to increase.

Section 8.2

1. Refer to the glossary.
2. It increased employers' power over workers. Because they treated workers unfairly, labor unions were formed.
3. American Federation of Labor-Congress of Industrial Organizations; represents millions of skilled and unskilled industrial workers
4. dropped because of employer opposition, changes in employment patterns, and negative public opinion
5. Employment has shifted from manufacturing jobs to service jobs. In response unions have introduced skill training and career development programs, and addressed quality of life in the workplace, worker involvement in job decision-

making, and day care availability. Also, they have
offered incentives such as life
and health insurance pro-
grams, retirement accounts,
legal services.

6. Examples may vary but
should reflect an understanding of the different organizations listed.

Section 8.3
1. Refer to the glossary.
2. negotiate with management
on issues relating to wages
and fringe benefits, working
conditions, job and union
security, and grievance
procedures
3. They are neutral third parties
who help to reach a contract
agreement.
4. Unions can strike and management can replace strikers,
refuse them building entry,
and through legal action, prohibit them from striking.
5. Answers will vary but should
reflect an understanding
of the methods used to
resolve disputes in union
negotiations.
6. Answers will vary but should
reflect an understanding of
the benefits and limitations of
each method. Opinions
should indicate whether or
not effectiveness varies based
on the industry or business
involved.

CHAPTER 9
Section 9.1
1. Refer to the glossary.
2. to make major purchases, to
pay large annual or semiannual bills, for unanticipated
expenses, for major long-term
expenses, or to accumulate
money for security or leaving
an inheritance
3. savings account—pay interest
though it is relatively low;
money market account—
interest rates paid are higher
4. certificates of deposits—pay
higher interest rates than saving accounts for the money
deposited and purchaser can
select when they want the
deposit to mature from a
range of dates; saving
bonds—guaranteed by the
U.S. government funds, pur-
chasers buy them at for less
than face value and redeem
them at full value when they
mature, and they continue to
earn interest beyond the
maturity date until they are
redeemed
5. It decreases because money
that might have been saved is
consumed.
6. Students should find that
interest rates tend to be higher
when the bank is charging
them and lower when the
bank is paying them.

Section 9.2
1. Refer to the glossary.
2. loss of some purchasing
power in order to maintain or
increase future purchasing
power
3. helps to organize people's
wants and needs based on
their ability to pay for them
4. real investment; because it
increases the number of capital goods used by producers
5. Answers will vary but students should make an esti-
mated budget of their
expenses, earnings, and savings allotment. They should
also indicate what trade-offs
they can make to increase
their savings amount.
6. Answers will vary but should
show that a variety of services
are available for a range of
investors, from the novice to
the experienced. Students
should list what costs, if any,
are charged for using the
services.

Section 9.3
1. Refer to the glossary.
2. dividends and selling stock
at a higher price than it was
purchased
3. stocks purchased because
investors believe the corporation has good long-term
prospects and high-quality
products; because of their
long-term stability and value
4. bonds; because if company
fails, bondholders are paid
before stockholders
5. Answers will vary but should
reflect an understanding of
the advantages and disadvantages of online trading or
trading through a broker or an
investment bank. For example, in online trading
investors can see the bid and
ask prices but are offered no
trading advice and purchases
are not prioritized electroni-
cally. Trading through a
stockbroker or investment
bank, investors can seek trading advice and do not need to
follow the bid and ask prices,
but investors may have to pay
a fee for transactions.
6. If on the average stock prices
are rising, then we are in a
bull market. If they are
falling, then we are in a bear
market.

Section 9.4
1. Refer to the glossary.
2. advantage—people can buy
and use things without paying
for them with their own
money all at once; disadvantages—with loans, interest is
often charged and if loans are
not paid back, items can be
repossessed; with credit,
finance charges are applied to
the unpaid amounts of the
charge

3. to find out if applicants are high or low credit risks

4. If wisely used, credit increases consumer spending (demand) on goods services, which in turn drives up production (supply) to meet consumer demand.

5. Answers may vary. Students might respond that unwise spending can lead to credit debt and debt can be overcome with financial counseling and avoided by budgeting. Trade-offs could include sacrificing wants to avoid credit debt.

6. Students should list and compare different finance charges on three different credit card offers. They should list the type of credit card offered (VISA, MasterCard, gas card, etc.), the financial institution offering the card, the various interest rates the cards offer, and if the rates are promotional or not.

CHAPTER 10
Section 10.1
1. Refer to the glossary.
2. final output—to avoid counting products more than once; current year—so goods are only counted once, at the time they are made; and output produced within national borders—so only goods produced within U.S. borders are counted
3. by using nominal GDP and real GDP to show if production increased or decreased regardless of price
4. because GDP better reflects short-term resource use changes in the economy and many nations of the world use it
5. Answers will vary but provide relevant examples of national,

personal, and disposable personal income and explain why each example fall into each category. Examples might include corporate profits as national income, a paycheck before taxation as personal income, and a paycheck after taxes as disposable personal income.
6. Examples of "goods" might include leisure time and urban renewal because they improve society and "bads" might include pollution and traffic because they harm society or its standard of living. Some economists suggest assigning a positive dollar value to "goods" and a negative dollar value to "bads."

Section 10.2
1. Refer to the glossary.
2. Once the economy expands, it hits a peak and then eventually slows into a recession or a depression. The trough can follow, which eventually leads to a period of recovery followed by expansion.
3. If demand is low, then businesses might not invest in production to increase supply and a contraction can result. If demand is high, then production investments might grow to increase supply and economic expansion is encouraged.
4. affects amount of money in circulation by changing interest rate levels
5. Answers will vary. Students should indicate that if a recession looks imminent, they might curb their spending and save. If economic expansion is approaching, then they might increase their spending.
6. Students should indicate that the government works to maintain economic activity by

raising and lowering interest rates and taxes to encourage or curb spending and investment. They should find examples to support their findings.

Section 10.3
1. Refer to the glossary.
2. It helps to maintain a high standard of living, promotes effective competition in the global market, and provides the resources to deal with domestic problems.
3. increasing resources used in production or increasing productivity of those resources
4. through new technology, an enlarged, educated, and skilled workforce, and increased capital goods
5. Reasons include decreased savings and investment, decreased investment in research and development, increased government regulation, and the shift to a more service-oriented economy. Students should indicate which reason they support and why. Responses will vary.
6. Answers may vary but students should indicate that if their productivity falls, their grades will drop and their ability to compete with their class for the highest grade falls. If their productivity rises, their grades will rise, and they will present more competition among their classmates for the highest grade.

CHAPTER 11
Section 11.1
1. Refer to the glossary.
2. does not indicate differences in how hard people search for work, excludes marginally attached workers and discouraged workers, and does not represent the underemployed

3. Prices are stable when the unemployment rate is at a "natural" level. On the other hand, they say high levels of employment can lead to product price increases.
4. frictional unemployment; because it reflects workers' freedom of choice in the labor market and signals new jobs are becoming available in new industries
5. When unemployment is low (or employment is high), the economy is growing. When unemployment is high (or employment is low), the economy is slowing.
6. Depending on the unemployment rates, answers may vary. Students should indicate whether unemployment rate indicates that the economy is in a recession or expansion.

Section 11.2
1. Refer to the glossary.
2. Aggregate supply increases when price level is higher and aggregate demand increases when the process level is higher.
3. over 3 percent
4. Inflation affects the purchasing power of the dollar, the value of real wages, interest rates, saving and investing, and production costs.
5. Answers will vary but might include school supplies such as pens, calculators, notebooks, and folders because they are typical items that a student might buy for school.
6. Answers will vary but should include an example of product affected by inflation, such as gasoline, and by how much its price increased. Students should offer a valid explanation why the inflation occurred, such as increased production costs or aggregate

demand exceeded aggregate supply.

Section 11.3
1. Refer to the glossary.
2. Poverty threshold is the point before an individual or family is considered to be living in poverty. Poverty rate is the number of people who are living in poverty, or are under the poverty threshold.
3. The definition of income does not include deductions of expenses such as taxes, Medicare, and Social Security or the value of noncash benefits, such as food stamps and health benefits. Also, it does not account for different standards of living among families in the same income bracket.
4. changes in households, the labor market, employment and income, and the global economy
5. Opinions will vary but should reflect an understanding of different variables that could affect the income gap.
6. Answers will vary but should reflect an understanding that the market value of the goods and services a person has to offer affects income distribution, and if demand for the person's skills, education, and talents is low, that person's income will likely be lower than if demand were high.

CHAPTER 12
Section 12.1
1. Refer to the glossary.
2. homelessness and joblessness resulting from the Great Depression in the 1930s
3. grown in size and in areas such as education, heath care, and consumer protection
4. federal—insurance benefits and interest on debts

5. Examples include Medicaid and veterans' pensions. Such programs have grown because of rising poverty rates.
6. Responses should accurately reflect the student's state government's budget and describe how much is allotted for categories such as education and welfare.

Section 12.2
1. Refer to the glossary.
2. through rules and procedures enforced by agencies
3. It protects workers from discrimination, unfair treatment by employers, and unsafe working conditions. It protects consumers from unsafe products and unfair business practices. It also insures the money citizens' store in the bank.
4. funding and distributing them
5. Answers may vary. Students should recognize what programs improve the standard of living, such as health care, nutrition, and education, and what programs work to redistribute income such as Social Security.
6. It works alone to stabilize the economy because of the Constitution's mandate to promote the general welfare of the people. To accomplish this, it moderates the business cycle through actions such as changing taxation and spending policies. It also limits the effects of market failures through regulations and making information about market conditions available to the public.

Section 12.3
1. Refer to the glossary.
2. Government works to promote public interest through regulations and public

HRW material copyrighted under notice appearing earlier in this work.

policies. Also, promoting public interest, citizens can oppose government rules and policy by voting, political activism, and forming interest groups.

3. Prices usually increase, profits tend to drop, and productivity typically declines.

4. Regulation changes the way business is conducted by creating new rules businesses must follow.

5. Answers will vary but should reflect an understanding of the different methods individuals and groups use to influence and persuade others, as well as an understanding of interest groups and lobbyists.

6. Answers will vary but should reflect an understanding of interest groups and accurately describe a specific group's goals and activities.

CHAPTER 13
Section 13.1
1. Refer to the glossary.
2. allows consumers to compare prices, helps clarify opportunity costs, and provides a standard system of measurement for calculating expenses and profits
3. It is durable, portable, and stable. It can be divided into smaller parts and it is widely accepted.
4. Fiat money cannot be redeemed for specie or other commodity. Its value comes from government decree.
5. Answers may vary but should mention that the global economy depends on the widespread acceptance of money and might include that without it, the global economy today would collapse.

6. Answers may vary but should indicate five currencies and their value compared the to the U.S. dollar.

Section 13.2
1. Refer to the glossary.
2. brought order to monetary and banking systems in the U.S. and regulated charter banks
3. did not provide for an efficient method of regulating the amount of money circulating in the economy and lacked central organization
4. to regulate the circulation of currency in the economy and stabilize the currency values
5. overissue of currency or credit led to diminishing value of money; prohibited Federal Reserve banks from providing investment services and established the FDIC from to insure money stored in banks
6. The government bought all gold from banks so that a fund could be established to stabilize the value of the dollar. In turn, U.S. currency was no longer backed by gold. Answers may vary as to which countries also have eliminated the gold standard.

Section 13.3
1. Refer to the glossary.
2. automation, deregulation, and stabilization of the banking industry
3. lend money and accept deposits
4. through the Depository Institutions and Monetary Control Act, which eliminated many differences between financial institutions and enabled them to offer competing services
5. When many borrowers fail to pay back loans, banks lose assets and may not be able to

cover their accounts. An example might be how loan defaults contributed to the S&L crisis.
6. Students might answer that many banking services are available online, by phone, and through ATMs.

CHAPTER 14
Section 14.1
1. Refer to the glossary.
2. to control the amount of money in circulation and prevent the failure of banks
3. supervises member banks, holds cash reserves for lending to commercial banks or the government when needed, and controls monetary circulation to stabilize the economy
4. organized into national and district levels to spread the balance of financial control
5. The collapse of banks and endangerment of the monetary system changed people's attitudes. As result the Federal Reserve was established.
6. Answers will vary but should reflect an understanding of what the Federal Reserve is and indicate what types of decisions it has made and their impact on the economy, for example the decision to lower interest rates to stimulate the economy.

Section 14.2
1. Refer to the glossary.
2. They make transactions at local commercial banks faster and easier for the consumer.
3. The Fed manages the government's financial activities by acting as the government's bank, supervising member banks, and regulating national money supply.
4. M1—total of all currency in circulation plus the value of

all traveler's checks, all checking account deposits, and similar banking accounts; M2—total of M1 plus money market accounts, money market mutual fund shares, and other savings deposits with readily accessible funds; M3—total of M2 plus all large time deposits, purchase agreements, and some Euros

5. The phone company receives the $30 check and deposits it in its bank. The $30 is then paid to the phone company from its bank's reserves. Before the money is deducted for the student's account, the check goes through the district banks serving the areas of both the student and the phone company's bank. Each district bank is paid from reserves until the money is deducted from the student's account. Then the money is returned to the reserves.

6. The local bank will ship the worn bill to its district Federal Reserve bank in exchange for new notes.

Section 14.3

1. Refer to the glossary.
2. regulation of the amount of money and credit available in the economy
3. based on the amount of money people across the nation have and people's spending habits
4. margin requirements, credit regulation, and moral suasion
5. Answers will vary but should reflect an understanding of the challenges the Fed faces. Students should apply those challenges to their own life experience.
6. Answers will vary but should find information about easy-money and tight-money policies, the reserve requirement, the discount rate, or the prime rate and explain what they learned. Students could show how a topic affects an individual or an institution.

CHAPTER 15
Section 15.1

1. Refer to the glossary.
2. to pay for programs such as road construction, education, and national defense and to influence the behavior of individuals
3. proportional taxes—same percentage of income is taken from all individuals at all levels; progressive taxes—takes a larger percentage of income from high-income people than from low-income people; and regressive taxes—takes a larger percentage of income from high-income low-income people
4. individual income taxes, corporate income taxes, Social Security taxes, property taxes, and sales taxes
5. Answers may vary according to current state sales tax rules. In most states, jewelry is taxed, but milk and eggs are not. Sales tax is regressive because it does not take into account a person's income.
6. Answers will vary but should mention that property taxes are not based on a person's income.

Section 15.2

1. Refer to the glossary.
2. supply-side economics—tax reduction, deregulation; demand-side economics—an active government role in maintaining full employment and boosting business activity
3. to reduce unemployment, increase spending, limit inflation, encourage investment in new capital

4. timing problems, political pressures, unpredictable economic behaviors, and lack of coordination among government policies
5. Critics argue that supply-side economists' assumption of people's economic behaviors is not always accurate and that many tax cuts are unfair. Responses regarding opinion may vary but should reflect an understanding of supply-side and demand-side economics.
6. Answers may vary but should reflect an understanding of the different types of fiscal policy.

Section 15.3

1. Refer to the glossary.
2. The federal budget summarizes the ways in which the government uses fiscal policy.
3. wartime spending, increased corruption, and progressive reform; it is prepared by the president, who consults various advisers, then it is analyzed and approved or rejected by Congress, and then if approved by Congress, the president signs or vetoes it
4. to decrease high federal deficits and national debt
5. Some argue the benefits from deficit spending exceed the costs. Others argue that annual deficits and the national debt should be reduced so that money used for interest payments can be spent on national programs. Students' opinions may vary but should demonstrate an understanding of each argument.
6. Answers will vary but should reflect an understanding of the uses of and process

involved in creating the federal budget.

CHAPTER 16
Section 16.1
1. Refer to the glossary.
2. by determining ownership of production capital and the process of answering the questions of what, how, and for whom to produce
3. command capitalist system and command socialism—government; market socialist system and market capitalist system—individuals and enterprise
4. regulates decisions made by enterprise and owns capital used by the military
5. Decisions made did not reflect consumer preferences, did not make the most productive use of resources, and were based on ideology rather than the principal of economic efficiency.
6. Answers will vary but should reflect an understanding of the economic systems covered in the section.

Section 16.2
1. Refer to the glossary.
2. As the power of landowners declined and the power of merchants and monarch increased, new nations formed and grew in need of a national currency and banking system—two principles of capitalism. As trade and conquest rose to increase the wealth of early nations, governments maintained controlled tight control, which encouraged reform.
3. because even though France has a strong central government, which has controlled much of the economy, it has practiced indicative planning, which does not require private firms to base their economic decisions on the growth targets of France's economic plan
4. to direct resource allocation and production
5. A market capitalist economy was established in West Germany after Germany's defeat. East Germany operated under a command socialist system. When East Germany collapsed, large deficits resulted because of high unemployment of former East Germans combined with Germany's generous employment benefits. Yet, low inflation has been maintained with the help of Germany's central bank and growth is steady.
6. Answers will vary but should reflect an understanding of capitalism. Students should identify three capitalist nations and determine how long they have practiced capitalism and when they converted to a free-enterprise system.

Section 16.3
1. an entire society's ownership of the factors of production
2. to protect workers from harsh working conditions, to channel resources into socially desirable areas, and to oversee the distribution of wealth
3. Reformers challenged capitalism and encouraged it be replaced with socialism so that a more equal distribution of wealth would be provided.
4. It combined private industry with government-owned services; workers' enjoyed many economic freedoms; economic planning was controlled by representatives of public and private interests;

and high taxes financed social programs to increase quality of life of its entire society.
5. Answers will vary but should reflect an understanding of that political freedom and economic socialism are mutually exclusive. Examples include North Korea and Sweden.
6. Answers will vary but students should provide specific reasons why they do or do not support market socialism as a good basis for an ideal society.

Section 16.4
1. Refer to the glossary.
2. pure command socialism
3. Communism was not providing standards of living comparable to those provided by market-based economies; its lack of incentives resulted in decreased productivity; production decisions ignored consumer preferences, production costs, and the forces of supply and demand; and prices were not set based on supply and demand, which resulted in shortages.
4. Through the Four Modernizations, which targeted improvements in agriculture, industry, science and technology, and defense. Reforms called for state planning combined with market incentives to achieve the Four Modernizations and increase production. Reforms included the household responsibility system and free-trade zones.
5. He believed that owners of production resources oppressed laborers, which resulted in a class struggle throughout history. He proposed that a classless society without government would

emerge with the destruction of capitalism. Problems with his assumptions include a simplification of history and an inaccurate prediction of the benefits of capitalism and shortcomings of communism to the working class.

6. Answers may vary but might include that lack of incentives led to a fall in the economy's productivity.

CHAPTER 17
Section 17.1

1. Refer to the glossary.
2. developing nations—have low per capita GDP, limited resources, rapid population growth rates, and traditional agricultural or one-crop economies; developed nations—have a high level of industrial and technical expertise and a variety of economic institutions
3. dividing a nation's per capita gross national income by its total population
4. the production of just enough food for people to survive; surplus crop production usually is exported; and people tend to be isolated from the outside world
5. One explanation suggests that the increase stems from high birthrates, and another argues that medical and health care advances have increased human longevity.
6. Answers will vary but should illustrate an understanding of the role business or government policy plays in affecting a developing nation's economic development. Students might discuss the effects of business relocation in and on foreign nations as an example.

Section 17.2

1. Refer to the glossary.

2. scarcity and ineffective use of resources, inadequate infrastructure, political instability, and social and cultural resistance to change
3. inadequate education, job training, nutrition, medical care, unemployment, and underemployment
4. fear that business leaders' lack experience in determining what products to produce and how to produce them; few incentives for them to invest; instability of developing nations; and weaknesses in the economic infrastructure of developing nations
5. Answers will vary but should reflect an understanding of obstacles facing economic growth in developing nations. Examples may include offering incentives to encourage foreign investment or change government spending habits.
6. If people spend all their money trying to meet their basic needs, then they cannot save. Without domestic savings, capital formation is not possible.

Section 17.3

1. Refer to the glossary.
2. socialist model—centralized in the hands of national leaders; capitalist model—decentralized from the government
3. by increasing the quantity or enhancing the quality of their factors of production or improving their production technology
4. through the World Bank, the International Monetary Fund, the United Nations, and regional organizations
5. Experts question whether or not the recipients of foreign aid are receiving the maximum benefit. They suggest closer supervision by developed nations as a solution, but

recipients oppose this solution because of potential interference in their economic freedom. Support for either viewpoint will vary but should indicate an understanding of each argument.
6. Because a nation might not have all the resources to meet all its needs and wants, trade-offs become necessary. Answers regarding the types of trade-offs may vary. Examples might include choices related to spending on infrastructure, education, or technology.

CHAPTER 18
Section 18.1

1. Refer to the glossary.
2. It creates wealth and it allows nations to choose what they produce.
3. Comparative advantage determines how individuals and nations specialize.
4. the opportunity to become efficient in the production of a few goods and services and to trade them for whatever goods and services that nation cannot supply to its residents
5. Answers will vary. Students might answer that they would take into consideration absolute advantage, comparative advantage, and the availability of resources in making their decisions and should discuss reasons why.
6. Trade-offs occur when a nation decides not produce a good or service based on its comparative advantage.

Section 18.2

1. Refer to the glossary.
2. allows the international exchange of goods and services, tourism and travel, and investing by converting one nation's currency into another's

3. Because constant changes in international trade patterns, countries could not rely on it to maintain established exchange rates under the system.

4. current account—shows the dollar value of goods and services bought from and sold to other countries, the income that U.S. citizens and multinational corporations earned in other countries, and the income that foreign individuals and companies earned in the U.S.; capital account—keeps track of the flow of money between nations

5. When interest rates are higher, foreign capital increases. When they are lower, foreign capital tends to be invested in other nations.

6. by looking at the exchange rate; change from minute to minute

Section 18.3

1. Refer to the glossary.

2. tariffs, import quotas and voluntary restrictions, embargoes, and licensing requirements

3. political purposes

4. to reduce trade barriers and open international trade

5. Protectionists argue that foreign competition should be limited to protect young industries until they are fully developed, to increase growth of the domestic market, to maintain high wages and standard of living in the U.S., to limit overspecialization, and to maintain national security. They also believe that U.S. trade barriers should match those of other countries to keep trade fair. Answers will vary regarding which point of view students support. Students should explain their points of view.

6. The foreign corporation can avoid some shipping fees, tariffs, and quotas. The U.S. profits from increased employment opportunities and tax revenue from the foreign corporation's income, profits, and properties. However, trade issues have emerged as to whether or not products made by foreign companies in the U.S. should be considered "American made" and whether or not foreign businesses in the U.S. will outproduce domestic producers.